in full Bloom

"Claire Swinarski's *In Full Bloom* is rich with passion, truth, and encouragement. The battle cry of this book is a reminder to all Christian women that God has planted us where we are for a specific season or reason. Whatever that looks like for you, Jesus desires you to thrive, grow, and bloom as his disciple, and this book will help guide you in this growth."

Patty Breen
Catholic speaker and writer

"Claire Swinarski brings authenticity and practical wisdom to the process of becoming that we all find ourselves in. No matter what season, situation, or heart state you find yourself in, you will find encouragement and a kindred connection with her in this book. Grab a cup of coffee or tea and open to pages that will bring greater clarity and hope to your own journey of blooming where you are planted."

Sarah Kaczmarek
Director of Pastoral Ministry
Encounter Ministries

"*In Full Bloom* presents readers with a journey into the darkness of life, but instead of framing that darkness as a shadowy place of anxiety and fear, Claire Swinarski reminds us that sometimes the dark simply means that we are planted and waiting to bloom. Drawing upon her experiences, the wisdom of the saints, and inspirational stories, *In Full Bloom* is an encouraging read for anyone looking for a little hope."

Sr. Brittany Harrison, F.M.A.
Editorial and social media manager
Salesian Sisters, St. Joseph Province

"One of the things I love most about Claire Swinarski is her ability to be real, authentic, understanding, and challenging. In this book, she challenged me to cultivate a strong community, be fully present for the season in which God has placed me, and get off my butt and be an active participant as a disciple of Christ. Action, compassion, faith, and humor—she captured it all!"

Kathryn Whitaker
Catholic blogger, speaker, and author of *Live Big, Love Bigger*

FINDING THE GRACE
AND GRIT TO THRIVE
WHEREVER YOU'RE PLANTED

CLAIRE SWINARSKI

Ave Maria Press AVE Notre Dame, Indiana

Founded in 1865, Ave Maria Press is a ministry of the United States Province of Holy Cross.

www.avemariapress.com

Paperback: ISBN-13 978-1-64680-025-4

E-book: ISBN-13 978-1-64680-026-1

Cover image © Jeja/iStock.

Cover and text design by Brianna Dombo.

Printed and bound in the United States of America.

Library of Congress Cataloging-in-Publication Data
Names: Swinarski, Claire, author.
Title: In full bloom : finding the grace and grit to thrive wherever you're planted / Claire Swinarski.
Description: Notre Dame, Indiana : Ave Maria Press, 2020. | Includes bibliographical references. | Summary: "Claire Swinarski knows that the hard times and dull seasons are opportunities to grow. In Full Bloom inspires readers to see God's grace at work and discover for themselves the grit and practical strategies to thrive no matter what"-- Provided by publisher.
Identifiers: LCCN 2020023853 (print) | LCCN 2020023854 (ebook) | ISBN 9781646800254 (paperback) | ISBN 9781646800261 (ebook)
Subjects: LCSH: Catholic women--Religious life. | Women--Religious life. | Gardening--Religious aspects--Christianity.
Classification: LCC BX2353 .S955 2020 (print) | LCC BX2353 (ebook) | DDC 248.8/43--dc23
LC record available at https://lccn.loc.gov/2020023853
LC ebook record available at https://lccn.loc.gov/2020023854

for Krzys

Contents

Introduction

> NEW LIFE STARTS IN THE DARK.
> WHETHER IT IS A SEED IN THE
> GROUND, A BABY IN THE WOMB, OR
> JESUS IN THE TOMB, IT STARTS IN
> THE DARK.
> —BARBARA BROWN TAYLOR,
> *LEARNING TO WALK IN THE DARK*

Once upon a time, there was a girl who dreamed of ruling the world.

No, not like a queen or even a president. Not even necessarily the CEO of a Fortune 500 company. But a girl who dreamed of moving to New York City and *making something of herself*, whatever that's supposed to mean.

A girl who dreamed of pencil skirts, of heels clickity-clacking down the hallway of a skyscraper. Of a penthouse apartment and a well-behaved West Highland White Terrier, of children cared for by a French au pair and a handsome husband who did something bland, such as "work in finance." What *she* would do was more up in the air, but it was going to have an impressive sounding name, such as "human rights lawyer" or "vice president of marketing and communication." And of course, she'd write Newbery Medal–winning children's books on the side.

I had all of the makings of this life. All of the ambition. All of the privilege of a fully paid-for college tuition and a semi-sheltered upbringing. All of the support from a family that would cheer me on no matter what.

If I were to write out the timeline of my life and run my finger over it, the trajectory would amaze me.

Apathetic teenager.

Passionate political science major.

Campus missionary.

Wife.

Marketing assistant.

Unemployed marketing assistant.

Freelance copywriter.

Mother.

Wedding writer.

Podcaster.

Author.

None of these titles inspire television shows à la *The West Wing* or *Sex and the City*. None of these titles sum up the entirety of who I am, either. None of these titles were titles I dreamed of having (except, fine, author—I did always want to write books). But these titles are mine, each of them, some for a season and some for eternity. They are not what I expected. But they are what I have lived.

Many of us are facing titles we never expected. Some—mother, nun, executive assistant, dance instructor—may be joyful surprises, sweet blessings handed to us by the Lord. Titles we didn't dream of that God bestowed on us with a smile.

But some titles carry a heavy weight.

Sufferer of endometriosis. Resident of a place you don't want to live in. Single longer than you'd hoped. Fired. Rejected. Bored. Stifled. Failed.

Come on, sister. Grab a jacket. Let's go for a drive.

Let's roll down the windows and breathe in the fresh air, a gift given to us by God. Let's drive down to a large, clear lake, one where we can see our reflections. We'll clutch our iced coffees, tie our hair in messy buns, scrub the makeup from our faces. We'll walk down to the lake together and peer in, seeing one title that covers a multitude of savory or sad surprises: *disciple*.

To be a disciple is to walk alongside the Lord, and as the lake beats back and forth against the pier, it tells us a secret: *we can bloom as disciples no matter our season of life.*

My life right now is like nothing I could have ever imagined. I have two small kids who take up the vast majority of my day. They are exhausting and exhilarating; the best lessons the Lord could have given me. I'm married to a tall man from Poland who would rather read Tolkien than watch a basketball game. We live in a little brick house in the suburbs of Milwaukee, almost exactly an hour from where I grew up.

Why would anyone choose to live here? I must have asked my mom that a thousand times growing up. Wisconsin didn't seem an ideal location for a number of reasons. First of all, I was never one of those children that loved playing in the snow—I'll take days at the lake over wet socks and frozen eyelashes any day, thank you very much. Second, Wisconsin just seemed so *boring.* There were no cool companies, no beautiful old buildings. It wasn't New York, with its glamorous parades and premieres, or California, with its beaches that go on for miles and miles. It was farm, farm, college town, suburbs, farm, cute little town known for pottery, farm, farm, farm, Milwaukee, woods. The Packers were in there somewhere.

Mom would usually shrug and say the truth: *our family is here.* That's why I'm still in Wisconsin, against all odds: my family is here. I lived across the country from them for two years and knew that wasn't going to work for me.

But it's more than that, too. It's because it's where God has planted me.

It's where I'm *blooming.*

We've all heard women be compared to flowers, right? And it makes most of us cringe. But that's because we think of things with fragile petals and short life spans, tender things loved mostly for their beauty. I know, I know: garden metaphors! Really, Claire? Are you going to call us all pretty little daffodils, pat us on the shoulder while we pass out the key lime pie? But think of a *real* garden—the kind with thick vines, dangerously bright flowers, weeds creeping over and trying to strangle, plants fighting for oxygen and bursting through the broken soil.

Maybe you're not where you expected to be, figuratively or literally. Maybe you're not somewhere you *want* to be. Maybe you're in a season of transition or one of deep discomfort. But God has planted you there, for a reason or a season, and it's up to you to step into the role of discipleship and bloom.

But why does thriving matter? I mean, I seem to remember Jesus saying something about the downtrodden being blessed, right?

Jesus tells us in the Gospel of John that he came so our *joy* would be complete (Jn 15:11). I'm going to tell you something now, sister, that has taken me years to learn and that I have to remind myself of daily: *God wants us to live lives of joy.*

It's so simple to look at our own unfortunate circumstances and think, *This is the way it's meant to be.* We see the Cross and forget that three days later is a joyful Resurrection. We see the Lent and forget about the Easter.

We were not made to live every day waking up and wondering *when* God is going to deliver us to a new chapter instead of living the one we have this very moment. That does not bring us closer to heaven, it does not help us serve others, and it does not form our hearts into those of saints.

We are called to walk on a particular path, and that path isn't always easy. Our mama Mary knew that, right? She's the one I turn to when I need grit and perseverance the most. Being an unwed, pregnant teenager isn't a walk in the park now, and it wasn't then either. But Mary gave a fiat while speaking truth to power. When she spoke the words of her Magnificat—"He has thrown down the rulers from their thrones but lifted up the lowly. The hungry he has filled with good things; the rich he has sent away empty" (Lk 1:52–53)—I hear them as the charge of a Catholic feminist. Shannon Evans, one of my favorite Catholic writers, wrote,

> In my mind's eye, it's hard to imagine Mary demurely murmuring such radical statements with a shy smile and folded hands as she is so often depicted. These words are prophetic and powerful. My imagination is not Gospel of course, but it helps me personally to

imagine that her passionate delivery just might have caused a scene. However they passed her lips, these two seemingly simple lines indicate that even before Jesus walked the earth—even before his teaching, healing, and class-upsetting, even before he befriended the poor, dined with sinners, and had theological conversations with women—Mary already understood what God was about. She already knew that the kingdom of God is the great equalizer, disturbing social order and preferring the poor. Her conviction of this was likely one reason she would be qualified for the mighty task of raising the man who would flip everything upside down.[1]

Mary was blooming.

Pope Francis has said, "Sometimes these melancholic Christians' faces have more in common with pickled peppers than the *joy of having a beautiful life*."[2] Our beautiful lives have nothing to do with the size of our bank account or the health of our family and everything to do with the promises given to us by the one sent by God.

To wake up and truly be happy in my own circumstances is not something that I've always been good at. There have been times, as I'll share in this book, where choosing to bloom felt next to impossible. I don't dare attempt to guess the situation you find yourself in—the one that's breaking your heart, stomping out your seed, and stealing that joy like a thief in the night. But listen, sister: Here in Wisconsin? Our winter means piles of thick snow, freezing temperatures, and plants that will never see the light of day again. You look out onto that barren earth and think growth is impossible, for surely there is no life here.

And then in spring, there they are, all those signs of life. Plants and animals poking out little by little, doing their thing, reaching through the dirt and mud and sludge, relearning what it means to be alive, and turning their face to the sun.

I think you're here, holding this little book, reading my own twisting and tumultuous story, because you're ready to do the same.

Let's roll down the windows and let the sun in.

A NOTE ABOUT SOUL-CARE STEPS

At the end of every chapter, I want to give you some concrete action steps to put into place. Because here's the thing: we've all read a book that rocked us spiritually before we tucked it into our nightstand and never actually implemented anything it said. We are action-oriented by nature, sister. But the word "self-care" makes me think of fancy bath bombs and retreats with Gwyneth Paltrow, patron saint of crystals and weird medicinal trends. I also don't like the way the self-care industry tries to sell you a forty-five-dollar T-shirt before informing you that you need to #PutYourselfFirst. We were not designed to put ourselves first. The idea of caring for yourself at the expense of others does not match how Jesus lived. We believe in a God that asks us to go low so we can lift others higher.

However, in order to better serve the world with our gifts, we do need to fill our own souls with the love of Christ and the intentions of the Gospel. That's why we at *The Catholic Feminist* podcast tend to use the words "soul care." These are things that are good for your soul—that nurture you, help shape you, and treat you with the love God has for you. God does not want his soldiers run down, hungry, and unrested. He wants us performing at our best, in body and spirit. Hence the need for tender care for our anxious, uppity, fiery souls.

Part One

Planning Your Garden

HE HAS OTHER WAYS FOR OTHERS
TO FOLLOW HIM; ALL DO NOT GO BY
THE SAME PATH. IT IS FOR EACH OF
US TO LEARN THE PATH BY WHICH HE
REQUIRES US TO FOLLOW HIM, AND
TO FOLLOW HIM IN THAT PATH.
—ST. KATHARINE DREXEL

1.
Stuck in the Mud

When I woke up in a dorm bed that was supposedly a "tall" but was still a solid five inches too short, I knew I'd hit rock bottom.

My rock bottom didn't look like other people's, but it was uniquely mine: a pounding head, a fuzzy mouth, a missing roommate who was surely off studying after a night out. ("I do everything intensely. You should know this about me," Elle told me one of the first times we met. "I study intensely. I party intensely. I celebrate intensely. I'm just an intense person." She also does friendship intensely, which is why she's one of my nearest and dearest to this day.) It was fall but already cold; our ancient dorm building never felt properly heated, and my thin comforter picked up from Kohl's shortly before Welcome Week wasn't doing the trick. I missed my thick afghan from home, and that was it: the needle that broke this exhausted camel's back.

It was time to admit that I hated college.

I hate it here. That was the thought that popped into my head and wouldn't leave. I hated my stupid required classes, I hated the huge lecture halls, I hated the nasty dining hall food. I hated my too-small bed and the communal showers and the elevators that smelled like puke. I remember calling my mom, forever my support person when I was sobbing uncontrollably, and trying to problem solve. She's good in a crisis, good at talking out messy knots until they're smooth. Maybe I just had to stick it out. Maybe I had to drop a class. Maybe I had to transfer schools. Maybe I had to come home more on the weekends. It should be noted that my parents lived twenty minutes away from my dorm; truthfully, I likely needed

3

to go home *less* and spend more time adapting. But there were so many other things bubbling up under the issue. Yes, I hated the classes, and I was never really one for lecture-style learning, but it was more than that.

I was lonely. I was ridiculously, heartbreakingly, excruciatingly lonely. I had people to eat with in the dining hall, but I had no soul friends, like my lifelong best friend, who was living her best life at the University of Minnesota. Most of the people I spent time with were drunk on both freedom and crappy vodka bought with fake IDs. Just before school started, I had a friendship-ending disagreement with my only real friend that had chosen to go to college in our hometown, and from what I could see, he seemed to be absolutely loving college.

I was convinced there was something wrong with me. Why didn't I find this as fun as everyone else? Was I missing some kind of joy gene? Why did other people seem to suddenly have these large groups of friends, while I pretended that I wasn't feeling well so I could lay in bed and watch the Kardashians, not talking to anyone? Why was I waking up on Sunday mornings and not running off to the library with a big group of friends, wishing instead more than anything that I was curled up on my parents' sofa watching the Packers and looking through catalogues with my mom and sister, a fire crackling in the background?

But the University of Wisconsin had been somewhere I'd always wanted to go. I'd entertained the idea of other colleges, but I'd grown to love the city of Madison, and they had a great journalism program I was planning on applying to. The thought of transferring wasn't an option, either: I was already homesick and couldn't imagine relocating somewhere further. At the bare minimum, I knew my way around campus like the back of my hand. Being a University of Wisconsin Badger was in my blood. I didn't want to leave.

So I pushed through, spending as much time as possible at home and planning on moving into a ramshackle flat with one of my older brother's friends for sophomore year. But things just felt like they were getting worse. I spent the summer after my freshman year studying abroad in Australia, which didn't help the homesickness issue, and when I returned, I found that not living in the same dorm as my few college friends wasn't going to help the loneliness situation.

The first semester of sophomore year, I felt like someone was just stomping on me every single day. A boy broke my heart—although, knowing what I know now about love, I want to laugh and cry and give little Sophomore Claire a hug for the delusions of romance and heartbreak she had over *that* situation. My grandmother died. We had always been close, and she truly embodied my childhood in so many ways. Her missing presence made every single day feel more difficult. And then, the final blow: I was denied from the journalism program I had wanted so badly to study in. My reason for going to this university destroyed in a thin rejection letter. *We regret to inform you that your dreams are meaningless and your GPA sucks; perhaps consider putting down the tequila shot and picking up a textbook.*

If you were to look out the window on a Wisconsin January day, you'd see how I felt that year: Frozen. Barren. Honestly, pretty dead.

The silver sky didn't have any sunlight to shine down, and the plants were hiding deep down in the mud.

It was a dark, cold winter.

There was very little blooming happening.

At these times in our lives—when unbearably heavy loads weigh down our backs—the first thing we need to do is evaluate.

It sounds so cold and calculating, but I'm not talking about whipping out a pros and cons spreadsheet, although those can certainly be helpful. I'm talking about some good old-fashioned prayer. We need to turn to God and say, as plainly as possible, "This isn't looking how I want it to look. What should I do about it?"

Yes, this book is about blooming no matter where you're planted, about finding growth in unlikely places. But before we can get there, we need to know where we're supposed to be. Because the truth is, we don't want to use our circumstances as an excuse, either. When we're in a period of desolation, there are likely concrete changes we *can* make to our lives to change our circumstances.

Sure, maybe God wants you to grow through a season of homesickness by you staying where you are and establishing a community for yourself there. But, um, maybe he wants you to move home.

Or maybe God wants you to use your singleness as a time to start a nonprofit that will change lives. But he also might want you to sign up for CatholicMatch.

Sometimes God is yelling, "*Move!*" while we sit and try to figure out which type of glue we should use to stick our feet to the floor.

Before we can dive deep into blooming where we're planted, we have to make sure God doesn't want us to uproot a few things. Why do we need to start here? Because otherwise, I fear that you will read this book and hear it as a decree to live where you are, right now, no matter what.

But during that season of my life, God wanted me to adjust my trajectory. I had to do some inner work to figure out what was going wrong and how I could change my situation. It's like that age-old story about the man who is drowning but keeps insisting that God will save him even when an emergency plane comes to help. When he winds up in heaven, he's like, "What the heck, God? I thought you were going to save me!" And God's like, "Um, I tried. I sent you an emergency plane."

God sent me to a church community that helped me learn about him, make new friendships that would better my soul, and sort of shame me into boosting my GPA. I had to reorder my days and change the way I was living.[1] God wanted me to *change* something about my situation. He wanted me to change my actions, to undertake an external transformation in order to undergo an internal one.

Oftentimes, we jump immediately to how we can spiritually surrender to a situation. This is a move fraught with good intentions, but it's important that we also evaluate what small, actionable changes we can make to improve our lives. God wants to work *with* us. You can beg him for peace about your situation, but maybe you're just in a bad situation that you need to get out of.

Maybe you need to set up a boundary and end things with that boyfriend.

Maybe you need to leave that job that isn't paying you enough to get by.

Maybe you need to seek out a counselor that can walk you through some of your struggles with mental health.

Maybe you need to invest some money in a course that will teach you a new skill.

Jesus had a different direction for almost everyone he encountered. He asked the rich young man to sell everything he had and follow him (Mt 19:16–22). He approved of Zacchaeus's plan to make amends with the people he had wronged (Lk 19:1–10). He asked Peter to lead his Church (Mt 16:16–19). Instead of calling him to be a disciple, Jesus left John the Baptist to stay right where he was and keep going (Lk 3:15–22). Just because he is asking *this* person to do something does not mean that is *your* calling.

My friend Patty Breen is one of the most beautiful, courageous examples of this to me. She's a writer for Blessed is She as well as a Midwesterner with a passion for ministry. A few years ago, she sought a divorce and annulment after she realized she was in an unhealthy marriage.

"I never dreamed as a young Catholic woman I would find myself navigating these messy spaces in my story," Patty said. "I saw I was simply surviving and not thriving, and after much prayer and seeking counsel, I decided the only option I had left was to walk away. Afterward, I knew I needed deeper healing and wholeness. I needed to take responsibility for my part in our marriage's failure but also acknowledge all the things I dragged into marriage. I needed to process childhood wounds, traumas, and my own baggage."

Marriage is a vocation that in today's society is so often belittled and overlooked. It's no longer seen as an everlasting union but as one that can be easily tossed aside for a variety of reasons. The Catholic Church has been one of the greatest champions of marriage, insisting on the importance of family structures and providing resources in order to strengthen marriages. But there are times when marriages are not of God. There are times when the brave thing to do is not to stay but to ask God if you need to leave.

"I saw the annulment process as another tool to facilitate my own healing. In time, it helped me to choose to forgive my former husband and learn lessons about grace and mercy I never knew I needed. Catholics who experience the devastating pain of divorce are not outside the loving gaze of Jesus. He wants you to know he sees the whole of your experience, and Jesus wants you to experience healing," Patty explained.

Listen, sister. I'm not telling you to run for the door. I'm not telling you to radically change your entire life.

I'm telling you to do what Patty did.

I'm telling you to pray.

Prayer! Prayer is so underrated, maybe because it's not as Instagram worthy as attending a rally or artfully organizing your refrigerator. To sit in that quiet space of God, to allow him to speak in the silence of your heart, to ask of him what he needs from you and to respond—it's important work.

Prayer feels like inaction, what with the sitting and talking to someone you can't see and not getting to knock things off your to-do list at the end of it. I know it's cool these days to argue about offering prayers versus offering action. But so often, *prayer is action.* If you don't believe in the power of talking to our risen Lord, if you don't honestly think that asking him to move or make things clear is *action* or worth your time, then I need to point you back to the gospels. Remember that this is Jesus, who rose from the dead, who fed thousands with a loaf of bread, who made miracles happen. And even he took time away to pray, retreating from the crowds and allowing himself that time to speak to the Father. Jesus knew that prayer needed to be the root of all of his actions.

We have a God who desires to know and love us; in fact, his Son calls us his friends. How are we supposed to know what he wants us to do if we aren't talking to him?

If you are living in an abusive relationship, in desolate circumstances, or in the grip of addiction, I don't want you to read this book and walk away thinking, *Well, this is where I'm planted, so I guess I just need to pray more.* But I do want to impress upon you the vitality of a full, rich prayer life, one that looks like rosaries and running errands, one that's scripture in the morning and scrubbing dishes in the evening, one where you feel such a deep connection to God that you don't need the perfect prayer circumstances to be speaking to him in your heart.

I can't tell you if you're in a situation where you need to uproot or replant, if you're in a season of growth or death. I *can* tell you that

God hears prayers. I can tell you that there is power in a candle and a cup of coffee and a Bible, that the letters from Peter have changed me, that silence is a powerful wind of the Spirit. Just like Elijah was waiting to hear God in an earthquake and fire and eventually heard him in a whisper, so will we (1 Kgs 19:11–13). We think that God is hiding his will from us, but y'all—he *wants* us to do his will. He will make it known if we ask. He isn't hiding a neon sign under the covers, waiting for it to be revealed. He's longing to be in conversation with us.

Throughout this book, you will hear many stories of people that need to bloom where they're planted. But it's important first to consider whether you need to uproot, like Patty did. Whether you need to dig up a seed and begin again.

Patty told me that the annulment chapter of her life would not define her. That it was only a small piece of the wider tapestry God is designing with her life. That these years have had fruit, that they have helped her encourage other Catholic women feeling desperately alone in similar circumstances.

St. Joan of Arc tells us that if we act, "God will act."[2] I can tell you all of the things I will tell you in this book: that we can find sunlight even in the dreariest of seasons, we need time to flourish, and we need to stay connected to our roots. But if you're in the wrong garden, sister, none of this will resonate. Some plants just aren't going to make it in some soil. Try to grow some peonies in the middle of the New Mexican desert and tell me how that works out for you. God has a splendid design for our lives, an intricate plan for us to live with full, complete joy. He is not satisfied with us trying to spiritually tie ourselves to a situation that Isn't Right. He desires to empower us to make the changes we need to make. There is a saying that stagnant water becomes putrid. If we aren't growing, shifting, constantly evaluating where we're at in life, and seeking the face of Christ, we will become putrid, and we will not be living out the lives Christ intended for us to live.

Patty needed to seek an annulment. I needed to get my butt to a church. You may need to do something, too. You may even be in a system that is unjust or unfair, facing consequences from choices that were not yours or policies that are not of the Gospel. You may be facing real, true struggle, and me telling you to try and bloom feels like a slap in the face.

The choice isn't whether to thrive where you are or change your situation. The truth is that you can do both. You can fight to improve your circumstances while accepting your day-to-day. Living each day as if *that day* is God's will for you, all the while striving toward an ultimate path, is a Gospel-centered blooming, not the tepid, temporary #DreamLife so often shown by reality stars or mommy bloggers. It's a type of blooming that requires a commitment to seeking Christ in all people, even yourself.

Action takes bravery, sister. Pope Francis has said that "we cannot be tepid disciples. The Church needs our courage in order to give witness to truth."[3] And we can feel so very uncourageous, so very little.

Good thing we have a very big God.

SOUL-CARE STEPS

* **Make a prayer plan.** Schedule it in, sister. When I was a FOCUS missionary, I used to literally sit with my disciples and write out their prayer plans in their planners. If you don't plan it, it ain't getting done, but you *will* find time to binge-watch three seasons of *The Great British Baking Show*.

* **Text a friend.** Who's in your corner? I know that for many of us, this list may be short or spread across the country. But who in your life is the person you can turn to in a spiritual crisis? Text your mom, former FOCUS discipler, Bible-study leader, friend from high school, whoever, and ask if they can get together for coffee—in person or virtually—sometime this month. (And if you want to make it margaritas instead, nobody in these parts will judge you.) Tell them how you've been feeling lately with this season of life and see if they have any valuable insight. It's vital to make sure this is a person who is *for* you, meaning *for* your salvation—not the kind of friend who's just going to suggest a pedicure, although those friends are great, too. A friend who knows your heart and is in the corner of

Christ—that's who we need in these tricky, trying seasons. When we're feeling overwhelmed, it's so easy to hide, isn't it? But we need to wipe away the dirt and dig our hands into the soil. We need to uncover our roots and look at the hard truths. And the people in our lives can help us do just that.

* **Consider which doors are open.** If you apply to a spiritual community and are rejected, that's a pretty great sign that that isn't where you're meant to go. If you want to move to San Francisco but are barely making rent in small-town Iowa, that's a solid arrow pointing you far away from an expensive housing market. *I just feel like I'm meant to marry him*—let me take your hands, look you in the eyes, and remind you that if he is choosing no, that is the truth of the matter. Knowing what options are actually available to you is incredibly helpful when deciding on your next steps. If you literally can't change your situation, that helps you know that God *isn't* asking you to uproot. Don't worry if that's you, sister—you're in the right place.

2.
Looking under the Soil

When my husband and I bought our house, it was the dead of a cold Wisconsin winter. It was the kind of winter where you could see your breath as soon as you woke up in the morning; the kind of winter where you poured pots of boiling water on your garage door in order to unfreeze it. A winter of thick socks and hot tea. We saw the recently remodeled kitchen, the beautiful paint colors, and the carpeted basement. We saw a cozy windowsill perfect for a reading nook and the cabinet space galore. We saw the attached garage, a thing of beauty for any mom with toddlers who needs to hit up a drive-through on a rainy day.

What we didn't see was the yard, covered in a thick foot of snow.

When the spring finally came and the snow melted away, things were a mess. Don't get me wrong—it's Wisconsin in the spring. *Everything* is a mess. I think the psalmist who wrote about walking "through the valley of the shadow of death" may have been thinking of the gray pit of sludgy hell that is a Midwestern spring. But our yard in particular was covered in weeds. There were long stretches of garden in our front yard and backyard filled with tangled, neglected plants, and thick shrubs of weed covered every patch of soil. The dead leaves nobody had raked in the fall were frozen, caked into the lawn under wet layers of mud. The grass was barely grass; it was mainly large patches of creeping Charlie and dandelions. "This yard," my mom told me frankly, "looks like nobody has touched it in two years."

This was terrifying for a number of reasons. The first was that one of the main reasons we had bought a house was our desire for a yard. Apartment life was growing old, and we were convinced our two kids needed that All-American Backyard Vibe. The yard was big, but now all I could think was that the large yard we had been so excited about meant a large piece of land I suddenly needed to maintain. Furthermore, I had no idea where to start. Can you rake in the spring? How do you even make grass grow? Is that a plant or a weed? What about that? What about *that*?

I wanted to snap my fingers and have the kind of garden Joanna Gaines puts on Instagram, with beautiful flowers we could gift to friends, herbs we could use in our own homemade meals, and a backyard with lush, green grass where our kids could get their feet dirty. A backyard that resembled the one on *Parenthood*. I wanted the kind of home where kids could run themselves ragged in the twilight, safe and protected in the jungle of their own backyard.

But that is not what I had. I had a limited budget, even more limited knowledge, and a busy summer filled with book deadlines and children and family vacations. The odds of me having that Dream Backyard were slim to nil.

It was tempting to just shut the windows and say, well, we don't have time for the yard of our dreams right now. Maybe next year.

Instead, here's what we did.

I asked my mom to come over and literally tell me what was a weed and what wasn't. My husband, Krzys, dug a long trench across our front yard so we could bury the ugly black water pipe the melting snow had revealed. We pulled up weeds, we spread some soil, and I put flowers in the beautiful planter the people before us had left behind.

Basically, we planted seeds.

Seeds take *time* to grow. Planting them isn't an instant fix. There was nothing I could do to make that backyard the way I wanted even after an entire summer of work. Because these things take time. This was not the season for the Backyard of My Dreams.

Instead, it was the season for perfect imperfection. There were plenty of nights where I sat under our Target-purchased twinkle lights and stared at the piles of weeds that still needed eliminating. But there I sat. I sat not in the beautiful, remodeled kitchen, but on that rickety porch, the one that badly needed boards nailed down and a heavy dose of Raid sprayed underneath. I sat in that imperfect beauty and invited people to join me. Together, we celebrated the ministry of a chilly, bright summer night, of friends bringing over chips and salsa and cousins arguing over taking turns in a plastic Jeep pushed over tree roots.

Those seeds we planted, both literal and figurative, were a *start*. They were the steps we wanted to take in the direction we wanted to go, even if they weren't the size I wished they were or had the immediate impact I longed for.

In your current season, how can you plant seeds that will help you become the person you eventually want to be? In fact, there are probably things you can do that are perfectly suited for your season in a unique way.

For example, if you're in a job you can't stand and really want to grow your Etsy shop to become your full-time income, maybe there's a way your current job can help you learn the skills you'll need when you transition to being a full-time Etsy artist. Could you ask for more responsibility on your marketing team so that you learn how to do things like craft effective social-media copy? How could you plant the seeds that help you down the road?

Or maybe you'd really like to get involved in a pregnancy help center, but you live in an area where everyone around you seems to be riding the pro-choice train. Wouldn't this be a great time to practice having difficult conversations with people who think differently from you, a skill that would be incredibly helpful when you're eventually able to volunteer at such a center?

Perhaps you're struggling to have kids. The cross of infertility is a backbreakingly heavy one. It can feel as if moving through the world is like pushing through mud, trying to reach an end goal you have no power over. This patience, this waiting, this surrender to God—these are things that will one day make you a wonderful mother, whether a biological mother, an adoptive mother, a foster mother, or a spiritual mother.

These struggles, these difficulties—no matter what they are, they refine us. That refining is painful. But God can bring good out of any situation, any darkness, any difficulty. There are always seeds that we can sow.

One of my best friends, Marissa, came on the podcast in 2017 to talk about singleness. Marissa is a nurse who feels called to marriage but hasn't yet found the man she's supposed to marry. This tension between call and current reality can be difficult, particularly in Catholic Land, where people get married a bit quicker than the average couple (we literally used to refer to "June-October-Mays" in FOCUS, where you met in June, got engaged in October, and got married in May). Marissa said that she's been trying to ask the Lord how she can use *this* time to the best of her ability. She described using her spare time to visit friends and family and focusing on how she wants her life to look instead of who she wishes was in her life. I admired her perspective because I think the season of waiting in singleness is so uniquely difficult: a concrete example of desiring your life to look one way and instead having it look another. But she's still using her time well and planting seeds, growing in holiness to be the woman that God created her to be. She feels strongly that her vocational call is to marriage, so when she meets her future husband, her time spent becoming holier will help her be the kind of wife he deserves. But even if she or another single person who feels called to marriage remains single, the growing isn't for nothing. It's worthwhile for its own sake, and it's worthwhile for our sakes—even if it's not for the reason we initially planted the seeds.

It's easy to look out over our disastrous lawns, our heavy situations, and see only the dirt. To see no potential for any seeds to be planted. It's easy to think such things as,

Why bother dating? I live in a small town with zero Catholic men.

Why send out job applications? I got fired from my last position; nobody's even going to look at me twice.

Why try to get pregnant again? I've miscarried more than once, and my body is clearly broken beyond repair.

I looked at those weeds, that dirt and muck, and saw nothing but nastiness. I had to make myself look deeper, closer, put my face up to the soil and observe what was really going on.

This is an important step that gardeners take every spring: they plan. They figure out the soil type, they look up the last frost date in the almanac, and they plan out what they're going to plant and when. They assess their current situation and make a plan of action for what to do next. If you skip this step and go right to planting seeds, who knows what you're going to miss?

Before we do any type of planning, I'm going to give you that cliché command any Christian worth their salt deals out. We need to take the time to pray. I know, I know—you're thinking, *Wasn't prayer her prescription in the* last *chapter?* Yes, it was, because it's vital for every part of the process. Not just at the beginning, when you're deciding if you're going to make changes, but also once you've decided to make changes or stay put, prayer remains an essential piece of the puzzle. Some of us struggle with dragging our feet and avoiding action steps, while others of us (that is, me) struggle with diving headfirst into change without consulting the Good Shepherd. When we wake up and feel like our life is a bit of a mess, it's tempting to dive into changing every single area at once. But that isn't sustainable or effective. It only leads to burnout. We need to prayerfully ask God which direction he wants us to go before we begin. Is God's direction for us always crystal clear? No. I know I'm not alone in wishing neon signs from Jesus were more of a thing. But if we're praying, we at least know we're in communication with him; we've asked him to guide us where he wants us to go, and we know he's with us. St. Augustine told us to "love God and do as you will."[1] We don't need a handwritten letter from Jesus Christ Our Savior to put an action plan in place. But we *do* need to be walking with him in prayer.

In the Gospel of Mark, when Jesus tells us the parable of the sower, he describes a person laying seeds. Specifically, he focuses on the type of ground the seeds fell on, because where we lay our seeds matters. He says, "Some seed fell along the path, and the birds came and ate it up. Other seed fell on rocky ground where it had little soil. It sprang up at once because the soil was not deep. And when the sun rose, it was scorched and it withered for lack of roots. Some seed fell among thorns, and the thorns grew up and choked it, and it produced no grain. And some seed fell on rich soil and produced fruit. It came up and grew and yielded thirty, sixty, and a hundredfold" (Mk 4:4–8).

No matter how we're living our lives, we're laying seeds for who we truly are. The small decisions we make, the minute interactions we have with others? Those are all instances of us planting seeds, and they're either going to fall on bad ground, tearing us further from who the person of Jesus has called us to be, or they're going to fall into good soil and produce grain.

Deciding to live our days in bitterness or in anxious anticipation—those are dropping seeds into rocky ground. Those choices are investments into a life that we don't want to be living. You do not want to look back on these wild, precious years and remember that you spent them Instagram stalking that guy, obsessing over that frustrating neighbor, or Googling every diagnosis you can find on WebMD, the same way I didn't want to look back on our summer and realize I spent it sitting indoors. We want to invest in a faithful, fruitful, and fulfilling life. Because that's the one Jesus designed for us.

The key word in that last paragraph? *Deciding.*

Those small steps and decisions can be some of the hardest ones to make. Even with my silly backyard example, it was so hard to convince myself to go outside and weed that stupid thing. Because instead of it being one giant project I could complete and then be done with, it was instead going to be thirty minutes here, twenty minutes there, and then a stolen hour or two the following weekend.

But little by little, those small steps added up to something great.

What if all of the saints who walked before us had waited for perfect timing to begin growing closer to Jesus? What if they used the excuse of less-than-ideal circumstances to stay stuck instead of growing, stretching, and thriving?

In our own lives, we can't always do the "great" thing.

We can't get married just because we want to.

We can't get a new job just because we want to.

We can't go on pilgrimage, get a book deal, or heal from a devastating illness just because we want to. We can't bring back relationships that have ended just because we *want* to.

But those small seeds of virtue? We can consistently plant those. Those are the things we have control over: getting up every day and going out into our own metaphorical (or literal) garden. And when we sow those small seeds with great love, we *are* doing great things. Even when they yield fruit we weren't expecting when we planted them.

For example, I used to think being a missionary meant being one, well, *professionally.* To have that on a business card or your Facebook career description. Spending two years as a campus missionary made me feel like I was spending my day-to-day life doing something important.

But after I left full-time mission work, I found it hard to see how I was forming disciples. I was spending most of my day trying to get writing published and keeping a very cranky baby alive. I wanted to be out there in a real *mission field*, but I felt like I couldn't: after all, I was a mom and a wife, I had a home and a job.

At the same time, just because I wasn't doing professional, full-time mission work doesn't mean I couldn't be on mission. I still found ways to share the faith, such as through having intentional conversations with friends, practicing daily intercessory prayer, and starting *The Catholic Feminist* podcast. Do those small seeds look like the glamorous life of a *missionary*? No. But was I sewing small seeds of mission everywhere I went? Absolutely.

As I was working on my backyard, trying to learn what was weed and what was flower, there was one large plant I nearly pulled out of the ground before my mom stopped me.

"Don't you know what that *is*?" she told me excitedly. "That's rhubarb! You have rhubarb!"

That "weed" I almost eliminated from our backyard was a sweet, tangy fruit, perfect for crumble and pie, an easy gift to hand to visiting friends and one that kept blooming all summer long. Thank God someone told me. Thank God someone *looked*.

The hard truth is this, sister: we cannot jump straight to the dahlias and daffodils.

But no matter where we are in life, we can be planting seeds that will eventually grow into a garden of abundance.

And sometimes there's fruit already growing in our lives that we didn't expect. We just need to look.

SOUL-CARE STEPS

* **Evaluate your grass.** What kind of spiritual yard are you tending? Is it in pretty good shape and just needs some pruning? Are there any really gray, slushy spots you think are beyond repair? Before you can begin implementing any type of change, you need to assess your current situation.
* **Prayerfully prepare.** Ask God to place on your heart what he wants you to do. Even if you don't get a clear-as-day response from your prayers, know that as long as you remain in communion with him, his will can be revealed.
* **Go seed shopping.** You can't just run to the garden store and pick up the cutest packets; you need to learn about your own area, your own weather, and your own soil. Check out a few different types of "seeds"—actions that will help you start making meaningful change—and decide which would be perfect for your unique situation. Maybe you need to invest in a new online course to kick-start your career, find regular childcare so you can attend adoration and deepen your faith, or start attending young adult events for local Catholics in your area to build community.
* **Get in the dirt.** Any positive change is going to require a level of sacrifice. It may be as large as moving across the world or as small as eliminating a bad habit. But it will require grit, grace, and gumption.

Part Two

Planting Your Seeds

HOLINESS CONSISTS SIMPLY IN
DOING GOD'S WILL, AND BEING
JUST WHAT GOD WANTS US TO BE.
—ST. THÉRÈSE OF LISIEUX

3.
Developing Good Routines

Let's talk about Jesus.

Oh, man, I hear you thinking, *the Catholic girl's going off about Jesus.* Look, I used to be a missionary. Old habits die hard. But I am an evangelist in the purest sense of the word: I share about things I love. If I try the new latte flavor at Starbucks, best believe I'm all over Instagram Stories blabbing about it. If the newest Netflix documentary on some type of scam is a hit, I will scream about it for miles. (You guys, the one on the Fyre Festival? It was my love language.) When it comes to the people in my life, I will gush about my friends, talk up my family, publicly praise my husband, and brag on my children.

And I do love me some Jesus.

His followers, both biblical and current? They can drive me absolutely insane. But Jesus, the carpenter, the friend, the son of God. Jesus, who used stories to point people to truth? Jesus, who invited the outcasts to dinner and spoke truth to power? Jesus, who doled out forgiveness unflinchingly, who wept at the death of a friend? Jesus, fully human, fully God, fully ours?

We start with Jesus.

We don't start with the theology behind consubstantiality, Gregorian chants, or, like, Leviticus. We start with the man.

If we're going to truly bloom at any point, at any place, we know that we need our roots to be deep within the earth. If you try to replant a flower but don't properly bury the roots, they won't grow into the soil, and it won't truly flourish. For us, Jesus is our earth. We need to be rooted in him, otherwise all our hard work won't amount to much. Just like in the parable of the Sower (Mk 4:4–8), we have to make sure our seeds are falling on good soil: the soil of Christ.

Jesus tells us in John:

> I am the true vine, and my Father is the vine grower. He takes away every branch in me that does not bear fruit, and every one that does he prunes so that it bears more fruit. You are already pruned because of the word that I spoke to you. Remain in me, as I remain in you. Just as a branch cannot bear fruit on its own unless it remains on the vine, so neither can you unless you remain in me. I am the vine, you are the branches. Whoever remains in me and I in him will bear much fruit, because without me you can do nothing. Anyone who does not remain in me will be thrown out like a branch and wither; people will gather them and throw them into a fire and they will be burned. If you remain in me and my words remain in you, ask for whatever you want and it will be done for you. By this is my Father glorified, that you bear much fruit and become my disciples. (Jn 15:1–8)

The branches can't be disconnected from the vine and still bear fruit. If the cause for our routine is anything less than Jesus, it isn't going to flourish. The cause could be any very, very good thing—our marriage, our devotion to a nonprofit, our education. But anything less than Jesus is unacceptable. He wants us entirely.

Luckily for us, our God is everywhere. He's in the streets and the sanctuaries, the offices and the nursery schools, the apartment buildings and the dorm rooms, the kitchens and the warehouses. So long as we root them in him, he's even in our very, very good things—our marriage, our devotion to a nonprofit, our desire for education. Our God does not sit still. Therefore, we *can* remain connected to the vine no matter our life circumstances.

The question is if we will choose to.

I've had the opportunity to speak to many Protestant women through my work as a missionary and now podcaster. *The Catholic Feminist* has a great deal of Protestant listeners, and I'm so grateful for their wisdom and insight. I also listen to plenty of podcasts hosted by Protestant women, such as the *Upside Down Podcast* or *The Happy Hour with Jamie Ivey*. I believe our Protestant sisters can know, love, and serve Jesus.

But there's something about our Catholic faith that I need to give thanks for in this space, and that is its material nature.

Catholicism has routines. Routines: we love them, we cling to them, and we wave them like flags. They're sometimes called dry or dull, they're often belittled, and they're even criticized as being too "High Church." But as Catholics, we believe in the sacredness of routine. We believe in the miracle of doing the same thing over and over again and imprinting it onto our hearts.

That's why we have the Mass, where the same readings are read across the nations in thousands of languages. That's why we have the Rosary, where together thousands of us can run our fingers across beads and beg Mary for aid. That's why we have the Liturgy of the Hours, where we can mark the passing of days with prayer. That's why we have the St. Michael Prayer, where together we can call down the powerful force of light. That's why we have Confession, Baptism, and the other sacraments, where we can reap the graces of Christ. We believe in the power that comes from doing things together. Yes, you need an individual relationship with God. And of course different people will feel closer to God through different rituals. But there is something to be said for a group of people chanting the Our Father in unison, not just whispering it alone. There is something that happens when a group of people receives Communion together instead of experiencing God in a lonely, individual way: we are made aware that together we are the Body of Christ (1 Cor 12:27). Fully God and fully man, Jesus walked on this earth, and we are fortunate enough to be able to unite with him through physical experiences.

When I was in college at the University of Wisconsin, there was an 8:00 a.m. Holy Hour. Every single morning at 8:00 a.m., the priest would expose the Eucharist. You'd be shocked at how many students were there, in rain or sunshine or (more likely) snow, unzipping coats and kneeling before Jesus. It was a routine that left us feeling united and grounded, a way to start the day that didn't have to do with exams, one that reminded us what was most important. No ministry is perfect, but I'm still incredibly close to many friends from college—even married to one of them—who all attended that 8:00 a.m. Holy Hour, and they are still, without a doubt, the holiest people I know. Not "holy" as in they all wear chapel veils and never cuss and wear knee-length skirts because #ModestIsHottest, but *truly* holy in that they know the face of Jesus and recognize him in others. I believe that's because they have spent so much time in his presence. (It also may be because that same priest advised all of us to go to Confession once every two weeks even if we didn't have any mortal sins, because venial sins can be like small bugs on a windshield—before you know it, you can't even see through it. Most of us still keep that habit.)

Throughout my time as a missionary, we were required to do a daily Holy Hour. Although sometimes frustrating—there were always more students to meet with, more mission partners to write newsletters to, more campus ministers to email, and this hour could have been filled with so many other things—the routine of Holy Hour was the bedrock of our ministry. It was the time we took to tend to our gardens and ensure that our roots were properly planted. That sacred routine kept me grounded no matter where I lived. Madison, New Orleans, Columbia—there I was every morning, on my knees in front of the consecrated host. And there I was every two weeks, going to Confession, exposing my soul and embarrassment. And there I was every Sunday, receiving the wine and giving the sign of peace. These rituals served as boundaries so that no matter what tumultuous waves were crashing through our often-bumbling attempts at ministry, we had a safe place to return. One of the first things I did with students as a missionary was invite them to partake in part of our Holy Hour. Then we would create weekly prayer goals and write them in their planners. We would make plans for afterward. I would hold them accountable, and they would hold me accountable, as people who love each other should.

Now my days look much different. I can't sit in front of the Eucharist daily for an hour—or, I *could*, but it wouldn't be prudent during this season of life with two small children, a full-time job, and eight hours of needed sleep, and prudence is an underrated virtue. I'm trying to be a saint here, not win the Holiest Mom on the Block Competition, and for me, my path to sainthood right now includes taking a step back from a full, daily hour of adoration. There are seasons in your life where you're unable to do the routines you're used to, and it can throw you off. Or it can make you meet God in new ways.

My new routine? I pray. I pray for fifteen minutes. Do I pray every single day? No. But I try. And I'm talking *prayer*—I'm talking sitting in silence, not flipping through scripture or reading the biography of a saint, as good as those things can be. Talking to Jesus Christ. Telling him why I'm dissatisfied or stressed, asking him to fix the cracks in the world, and speaking into him my hopes for the future. I try to read scripture daily and pray the Divine Mercy Chaplet weekly. My family attends Mass every Sunday and holy day, but not at all during the week, because while some people can handle two toddlers solo at Mass, I'm just not in that club. Krzys and I pray over our kids every night. These are the routines I cling to, the ones I return to when I'm in a fight with Krzys or late on a deadline or not feeling well. Or just, I don't know, not in the mood, but know I need to do something to reorient myself to God.

One of the most important routines I make sure to constantly stay connected to is that of regularly reading scripture. Jesus was a storyteller, as were the writers of the Bible, and the closer we cling to the Bible, the more we will be provided a road map of belief. As Sarah Mackenzie writes in *The Read-Aloud Family*,

> When we're telling our children the story of Jesus heal-ing Jairus's daughter, of curing the lepers, of raising Lazarus from the dead, we don't need to wrap up the story with a trite explanation about how God is pow-erful, good, or merciful. We don't have to add anything at all, because there it is—truth bubbling up out of the story. It *is* the story. When God pours down manna

> from the heavens, a child doesn't need to be told that
> he will provide what we need right when we need it and
> not a moment before. We simply read the story, and our
> children feel the truth of it in their bones.[1]

The stories in the Bible are powerful reminders of who God is, and by constantly turning back to them, we form our spirits the same way a child does when hearing them for the first time. There's always more to learn in scripture. We don't need to necessarily be part of a weekly Bible study or even have a formal Bible-reading plan, but regular scripture reading is one of the most important routines we can possibly embrace.

Pam Macalintal, a work-at-home mom living in Westchester County, New York, told me that praying in the shower is sometimes the only time she can carve out for prayer. I loved that: finding those times we are the most alone and being with Jesus instead. Stephanie Chludzinski, a high school theology teacher in Northville, Michigan, suffered a miscarriage and said she found the most comfort in turning to Mary in prayer, who certainly understands losing a child and has lived through the darkest of days. These routines, embedded in the daily moments of their different lives, keep them centered.

Your routine doesn't need to be completely, 100 percent made up of elements of the Catholic faith. Having some formal faith elements has been personally helpful for me, and I think it will be for you too. But in addition to partaking of the sacraments or prayer, a morning walk may be a good way to get your blood moving. A weekly phone call to Grandma can be radically transformative for your soul. When I moved to Missouri as a missionary, I immediately found a coffee shop I loved and a library within driving distance. I knew these small, material things would help me feel more at home, and visiting them quickly become part of my day-to-day life. Jesus wants us to care for our bodies and cultivate positive familial relationships. He wants us to love and feel loved.

I also try to form my other important routines to my current season of life. With two small kids, my husband and I can't go on date nights nearly as often as we'd like, but we *can* rent amazing movies and make fancy snacks for date nights in. I can't see faraway friends as much as I want to, but I can set up regular phone calls with them. Making your season work for you and celebrating what you *can* do will go a lot farther than mourning over routines you can no longer perform on a regular basis.

We have one enemy. It is not our circumstances or our Planned Parenthood–loving aunt or our uncle with the MAGA bumper sticker. It is the one who distorts what's in front of us so that we don't know which way to go. As Henry Cloud and John Townsend write, "Satan is the great distorter of reality. . . . There is always safety in the truth, whether it be knowing God's truth or knowing the truth about yourself."[2] These routines and rituals remind us of the truth of what *is* and not how things appear to us in the moment. By constantly knowing the truth about the world around us, we will be guided in our faith journeys. If someone gave you a map with places and roads labelled incorrectly on it, you'd never be able to figure out where to go. We look for maps in all kinds of places: evangelical megachurches, our offices, the Kardashians. We should be looking to our Church, but even that, at times, seems to lead us astray as we deal with the fallout from horrific abuse cover-ups or financial power taking precedence over people's souls and well-being. It's hard to know who to trust. Implementing a solid routine of faith keeps who to trust—Christ—front and center. And a solid routine for the areas of your life *not* directly related to faith helps support this as well. When we're feeling frazzled and undisciplined, we lose a sense of rootedness that allows us to lean further into the women we're meant to be.

The idea has often been floated that millennials are "unchurched" because they feel the Church is too focused on liturgy and not focused enough on serving. I've seen tweets and think pieces that go so far as to claim that those of us who are in our twenties would rather spend our Sunday mornings at a soup kitchen than in a wood-paneled church building.

Pardon my language, but I'm going to go ahead and call that a crock of shit. Millennials actually volunteer less than boomers or Gen Xers,[3] and before you come at me about millennials not having enough time or money, let me just point you to that part in the gospel where Jesus cheered on an old widow who gave her only coins to charity (Mk 12:41–44). I think the lack of churchgoing from millennials is because we distrust rules and restrictions. We are of the generation that didn't need a publisher to make our books; we could just pump one out on Amazon. We didn't need a movie studio to say yes to our film; we could create something on YouTube. We didn't need *permission* and we didn't need *leadership*, and while there is something beautiful and freeing in that, there is also something lost.

Because Church is more than a building. Church is who brings you casseroles when you have a baby and who watches that child when you have to go to the dentist. Church is who prays for you at Mass the day before your final exam, who gives you legal counsel pro bono, and who shows up with a pickup truck to help you move. Church brings over wine (or tequila) when you need to have a good cryfest about the trials of working-mom life or the difficulties of caring for an elderly parent. Church feeds you—literally with pizza nights and metaphorically with praise and worship. Church lends you the carving knife and throws you the bridal shower and holds your baby while you pee. Brené Brown says, "I went back to church thinking that it would be like an epidural, that it would take the pain away. . . . But faith and church wasn't an epidural for me at all; it was like a midwife. . . . I thought faith would say, 'I'll take away the pain and discomfort,' but what it ended up saying is, 'I'll sit with you in it.'"[4]

Church is also who challenges and helps you do these same things for others.

We *can* do our faith alone, but it is a watered-down faith; it is not the type of faith that truly encourages the growth we deserve. It's the wrong kind of soil. Sure, your plant might grow. But its potential is not nearly as high.

I say this knowing that many of you reading do not have this experience of church. Your church did not cherish; it shamed. Your church did not support; it tore down. Your church spent thousands of dollars on a surround sound system while you waited in line for food stamps. Your church has political signs on its lawn. In my line of work, I've had the opportunity to speak to many women who were deeply harmed by abusive church communities or the toxicity of purity culture. Or women who have no church but long for one.

Here's where I tell you the good news, sister: we are part of the *universal* Church. I may not be next to you in the pew, but I'm hearing that Gospel message right along with you. Your dear friend from college, the one who always made you feel confident in your faith and who now feels a million miles away, is accepting that same Eucharist. That priest who made such a difference in your life before moving to Rome is meditating on the same Rosary mysteries you are.

These routines don't just root us in Christ, they bind us together.

Sunday Mass may feel as dry as the desert to you. They may sing weird hymns from the '80s or chant in Latin or do any number of things you feel weird about. And hey, maybe you need to check out the church across town instead or join a different Bible study if the one you're in now doesn't really seem to be producing any fruit in your life. But find *something*. Find Church, and show up. The routine of showing up is the first step in being rooted.

SOUL-CARE STEPS

* **Look at your schedule.** Where can you fit in a spiritual routine? Do you have a lunch hour during the week where you could pop out to Mass? Does a parish down the road offer early morning Confessions? Could you listen to the Rosary while you walk back to your sorority house from the library at night?
* **Enlist a friend.** Accountability is key when it comes to routines. How many times would I have slept through that Holy Hour if a friend hadn't texted me first asking to grab breakfast after? Find a friend who can keep you accountable, even if it's a faraway friend you can only text. Don't just think, *Oh, I should text so-and-so and ask them to be accountability partners.* Stop and text them right now. That's what bookmarks are for.
* **Say the St. Michael Prayer.** Look, I'm not here to tell you what faith rituals to partake in, but I *am* going to tell you to say the St. Michael Prayer. It will take you literally ten seconds every

morning. It's a little intense ("Cast into hell *Satan*? Geez," my sister muttered to me as we recited it one Sunday). I know some of you prefer prayers about joy and light, not, um, hell. But the devil loves loneliness. He thrives in our uncertainty. In a time of blooming, we need to make sure we're constantly naming him and speaking the name of Jesus over him. So, the St. Michael Prayer. It's a daily must for me and my family.

> St. Michael the Archangel,
> defend us in battle,
> be our protection against the wickedness and snares
>   of the devil;
> may God rebuke him, we humbly pray;
> and do thou, O Prince of the heavenly host,
> by the power of God, cast into hell
> Satan and all the evil spirits
> who prowl through the world seeking the ruin of souls.
> Amen.

★ **Create a daily plan for a few key parts of your life.** It's not just our spiritual routines that need tending; it's our secular ones as well. Life will throw you curveballs you'll need to dodge, and things aren't always going to go according to plan. But having a set plan in place allows you to deviate from the plan when needed while still becoming the person you want to be. Spend some time in prayer and ask God where he wants you to focus: Your health? Your finances? Your relationships? Then implement some solid routines around those things. This could look like anything from committing to a Sunday meal prep to making it a goal to call your grandma at her nursing home twice a week.

4.
Planting a Perspective

We all have that friend.

You know when you've had a really crappy day? The kind when you're about to fall apart at the seams because two of your kids have an ear infection and you're two days late on that deadline already and you sense your period coming on and the fridge decided to randomly stop working because apparently Satan has declared a pox upon your house? And you're with that friend, venting, letting loose an emotional stream of consciousness about how life is *the worst* and everything is *terrible*? And she's nodding, sipping her coffee, and then casually lets slip, "I read a really interesting article about Haitian orphans today"?

Really, Susan?

But here's the part where I tell you something you may not want to hear.

Susan does kind of have a point.

I went through a period of time where every time I handed over my credit card, I froze. It was during those three months when everyone cared about Syrian refugees, before the media found someone else to feature and we all forgot about the millions of displaced people coming from a war-torn country. But every time I bought a latte or diapers or gas for my car or new pens, I got this sinking feeling that somewhere there was someone going without. Not just without their favorite type of Flair pen, but really, truly *without*: without food, without shelter, without diapers. Someone's child was hungry and wasn't getting anything at all, let alone Annie's Organic Gummy Bunny Fruit Snacks. Someone's stomach was empty, and they couldn't swing through the Chick-fil-A drive-through.

Here is where we as Christians live in an uncomfortable tension. The truth is, we as the Body of Christ are a dysfunctional family. Some of our siblings drive Teslas, and some of our siblings don't have a roof over their heads. Some of our siblings are poor, like, they can't afford the organic bananas, and some of our siblings are poor, like, they can't afford food.

I have an iPhone. I'm typing this on a MacBook. I'm at a coffee shop where I just paid three dollars for a cinnamon roll and ordered groceries online, happily plunking down the five-dollar pickup fee. I'm wearing a jacket I got from Stitch Fix because whoever's in charge of the thermostat here didn't get the memo that it's winter and the heat isn't high enough. This morning I went to the dentist and didn't bat an eye when asked for my dental insurance information. My Toyota is in the parking lot. I have a literal diamond on my finger.

I remember reading *Of Mess and Moxie* by Jen Hatmaker and feeling so seen when she told a story about being invited to a pool party while she was on a mission trip. A text from a friend dinged on her phone, making plans for salsa and swimsuits. She wrote that half of her was all, *American privilege, gross*, and the other half was all, *I'm so buying a new bathing suit for this!*[1]

That tension: it's strong and sticky. Because I can be all, *Wow, this friend really hurt my feelings with this comment, and I don't know if I should approach her about it*, and also, *There is someone who is going to go without food today, and she's right to be concerned about that.* It's hard to know if you can still be a passionate Catholic feminist while living a rich, full life, or if you're supposed to eschew all worldly pleasures for sackcloth and ashes.

There are two truths we need to hold in our heads.

The first is that our problems are real and that they matter. The same Jesus who hung on the Cross for our sins *does* care about the worries that plague us. He cares about your loneliness and your lack of sleep. He cares that you're anxious about your weight. He cares that you're unhappy with your medical school program, that you're sad you got passed up for that promotion, that you want to stay home with your kids but your family can't really make it work financially, or that the man you're dating isn't really the person you want to marry, but what if nobody else comes along and you've said a bunch of St. Thérèse novenas but aren't getting any roses?

The second is that someone, somewhere, does have bigger problems than you.

Full stop. If you have access to this book, your problems are not the worst in the world, which I understand is hard to accept and may be hitting a tender spot. Because your problems may be larger than any I have ever faced or ever will. But you have the knowledge of Christ, *and plenty of people don't.*

It's important that when we're holding our issues in perspective, though, that we keep a holy heart about it. Because there are a couple of issues with comparing our problems to the problems of those who have less.

First of all, we turn money into an idol, the ultimate Decider of Who Is Happy. Look, there are a lot of really happy poor people and a lot of really unhappy rich people. We decided money started aligning with happiness and lost sight of what truly makes people happy. I'm writing this during the Christmas season, and I recently reread Charles Dickens's *A Christmas Carol.* It's the most cliché statement of them all, that money can't buy happiness, but don't we all still need to hear it?

Second, we start to view people who have less money than us as some type of offensive monolith. In our mind, the stereotype of the "Haitian orphan" becomes a smear of people—usually people of color—whom we envision living miserably, in huts, with no ounce of joy in their pitiful lives. We use them to make ourselves feel better about what we do have, and anytime we're using other people to make ourselves feel better, we're running in the opposite direction of Christ. Are there people living that life? Certainly. But their role in life is not to make *us* feel better. Furthermore, many people living with far less money than we have, in circumstances we would consider far more dire, are perfectly happy. Jen Hatmaker writes in that same book that almost every family she visited in Ethiopia, many of whom we would consider dirt-poor, enjoyed delicious food and had some kind of art on their walls.

They played games with family members and complained about the weather.[2] In other words, *they really aren't that different from us.* They're not these stereotypes we can trot out when we're trying to put our problems into perspective. People living with less than us also love delicious salsa and board games and good music, okay? You're not some kind of Warrior for Truth because you bring up Starving Children in Africa every time someone complains. Life is not a ladder on which you can be higher or lower than anyone else. It's not a race in which this group of people are at the starting line and this handful seems to be at the finish and you're hanging out somewhere in the middle. You are where you are, and you can feel the way you want to feel about it.

Here is the whole truth, complex and messy: you are allowed to feel your feelings about your current life situation. Nobody gets to make you feel bad for feeling bad, okay? Your problem is real and hard and matters, no matter how small it may seem. Also, there are good things in your life, and you should feel thankful for those, even if they are the seemingly small securities of a roof over your head or a mom you can call and cry with or a best friend nearby. Those things can coexist. In fact, they must.

We could refuse to talk about our struggles, always pointing to people who seem to have less. But that wouldn't be the whole story. We could only lament our own life stages, refusing to be open to the fact that other people are suffering just as much as us with fewer resources. But that wouldn't be the whole story either.

Didn't Jesus tell us to care for the poor (Lk 14:12–14), and also tell a parable about gratitude (Lk 7:36–50), and also praise those who thirst for justice (Mt 5:6), and also tell us that God even cares for sparrows (Mt 6:25–34)? God both cares for us in our littleness and also requires us to turn and care about our brother or sister.

Jesus desires us to live abundantly, but we don't always under-stand what that *abundance* is supposed to look like. You heard about my vision in the introduction: plenty of money, a closet of Kate Spade purses, a few books I had written, with at least one winning a Newbery Medal, and maybe one extremely well-be-haved child. That is not the abundance I have. Instead, I have an abundance of grace. An abundance of poopy diapers and hugs, an abundance of cozy nights in, an abundance of laughter with my adult siblings, an abundance of adventure as I read library book after library book, an abundance of peace as I light a pine-scented candle and read the psalms when the house is still quiet and the heater is still kicking on. Abundance, everywhere, but not the type I imagined I'd one day have. Not by a long shot.

This perspective is powerful for us because it allows us to see things as they truly are. When we're in a season of life where we don't feel like we're thriving, it's easy to jump headfirst into a downward spiral, thinking, *Everything's a mess. My life is nothing like I hoped it would be. God doesn't hear me.* Such a perspective reminds us of important truths and helps us to see the world as God actually created it rather than being blinded by our own anxieties and worries. We cannot be who we're meant to be and set the world on fire, as St. Catherine of Siena directs us to, if we're constantly pointing toward our day-to-day problems.

It also helps us practice gratitude, something that will always be a central tenant of our faith. Giving thanks to God is something we so often forget to do when we're busy with our laundry list of requests. We forget to thank him for things as small as a beautiful sunset and as large as his unfailing mercy in Confession. Gratitude becomes something that feels just out of reach during difficult seasons, but that's all the more reason to reach for it. Anyone can have gratitude when they're living their dream life; when someone's day looks exactly how they'd like it to look, thanks flows easily. But when you're waking up every day and hitting the pavement with a heart full of sludge, in a season where nothing seems to be going the way you've prayed, the thought of saying "thank you" feels impossible. And those are the moments we're confronted most directly with where God is: he isn't found just in our happy days and completed to-do lists, in our promotions and our picture-perfect baby showers. He's found in the corners, the margins, the lowest levels of despair—in the rejection letters and the unwanted test results and the cross-country moves that take us away from everyone we love. There, too, is God.

We as Christian brothers and sisters cannot live with tunnel vision, so focused on our own concerns that we forget about the problems of the world around us. Yes, we need to stay focused on the Lamb of God, not political elephants or donkeys, but it's also our Christian responsibility to care for others. Something that made me realize this was the book *The Color of Compromise* by Jemar Tisby.[3] In his book, Tisby shows how saying that Christians needed to stay out of politics allowed them to delicately sidestep real-world issues impacting people around the globe and especially in America, from before the Civil War until now. "Staying out of politics" meant allowing slavery and racial inequities to prosper for centuries. In the same way, "staying out of politics" today means allowing women to be assaulted with rarely any legal consequences for those who attacked them, allowing unborn children to be killed in their mothers' bodies while laws support these deaths, and allowing people all around the world to starve while we worry how any government relief packages might impact our own taxes. Being aware of the world's problems means leaning *into* politics while still keeping the important truths in mind: that nobody can save us but Jesus, that it's up to *us* to act instead of waiting on the government to do something without us, and that if our brothers and sisters are hurting, we are, too. Mother Teresa is said to have asked God to "break my heart so completely that the whole world falls in." We should ask God to fill our hearts with the world, while still taking measures to keep our minds intact.

There have been times in my life where I've felt very, very lonely. Times when I felt there was not a person in the world who truly knew me or understood how I was feeling. I have not felt that way in a long time. And for that, I'm always given a breath of perspective from the Holy Spirit. Because when I need to sob my face off, I can call my husband or my mom or my sister; I can dial a circle of friends that knows my heart intimately. If I need to take one of my kids to the doctor, I have friends I can call who I know would drop everything at a moment's notice to watch the other. I have a support system standing behind me and catching me as I do the adult version of an awkward Church-retreat trust fall, and in my darkest moments of sadness, there is my thanksgiving.

Where is yours?

SOUL-CARE STEPS

* **Make a gratitude list.** Oh, it's corny! I'm sorry. But it's true: gratitude matters. Not only because it's what our faith tells us to practice, but because it truly can make you happier.[4]

* **Write a letter.** Turn off your phone, light a candle, find your favorite pen, and go old school with a handwritten letter to someone who has made a difference in your life. They may not live right next door during this season, but you can still express your gratitude for them.

* **Choose a cause.** Listen: I'm not telling you to pick a cause and throw yourself into it to distract yourself from your problems, and I'm certainly not telling you to use people who need help as a technique to make you feel better. But we were made to love other people. When we're doing that, we're becoming closer to who God made us to be. We were literally designed to serve (Gn 2:15). So by choosing a cause you care about and committing to it, you're taking steps toward sainthood and keeping a broad perspective that is aware of the world's needs. Whether it's emailing your local soup kitchen to inquire about when they need volunteers and then volunteering in those times, checking out a book about systemic racism from the library and using what you learn to change how you act or get involved in causes that draw attention to systemic racism, or setting up a monthly gift to your local pregnancy help center, finding a way to make a difference in your community can and will have an effect on your perspective.

Part Three

A Rooted Life

WE CANNOT LIVE AS CHRISTIANS
SEPARATE FROM THE ROCK WHO
IS CHRIST. HE GIVES US STRENGTH
AND STABILITY, BUT ALSO JOY AND
SERENITY.

—POPE FRANCIS

5.
Putting Down Roots

So is this the part where I tell you about New Orleans?

When I was twenty-one years old and crazy, I decided to become a FOCUS missionary. This plan was a strange one. I was graduating with a double degree in journalism and political science. I'd had communications internships with both a very influential politician and a major book publisher. I had a Dream, a Goal, a Five-Year Plan. It involved living in some sunny flat in New York, like Carrie Bradshaw's but with piles of books instead of closets of shoes. I'd write for some fancy magazine, until of course my fabulous novel career took off, and then I would just take long lunches with editors and talk about my next writing projects.

Then, you know.

God.

God is not a person you meet that changes everything; he's more the person that's always been there, patiently inviting you to find him, reminding you of his goodness when it seems no goodness can thrive. After being invited on a retreat by our college Catholic center, I went on it, and I made friends that would last a lifetime (well, I'm only twenty-eight, but things are looking good). I met Jesus slowly, through trips to adoration and acoustic guitars and washing dishes, and then I met him all at once, until I felt known and seen and all of those things the saints talk about. This person I had known about my whole life? I finally felt I *knew* him,

43

that the things he said could make a difference in my life. He was no longer some foreign concept but a living, breathing person, the embodiment of truth, a direction for me to walk in.

You know when you first start to kind of have a crush on someone, you want to bring them up randomly in conversation? Like, oh, I see you're breathing, you know who breathes *so* well? Jake from my geography class. Right?

That's how I felt with Jesus. That he had come so that we would have life to its fullest, and that so many of us were living these small, meager lives that were so much less than the ones he wanted for us. That I couldn't *not* talk about him. I was introduced to the Fellowship of Catholic University Students, also known as FOCUS, which is a campus ministry group that trains college students to share the faith. While I was in college, so much of my faith was poured into me by a FOCUS missionary that when she invited me to interview, I said yes, but was thinking in the back of my mind, *I'll do this interview for her, as a friend, before moving out to New York and living my dream life.*

This #DreamLife idea is such a farce, but don't we all sit around and pin images that look like our dreams? Whether it's the five kids we envision having or the career we've been after since kindergarten or the travel we'll do by ourselves around the globe, we have this idea that once we get There, we'll be Happy. That was certainly how I felt about post-college life. That once I arrived and found that mountain peak, things would be smooth sailing from there on out. It's so easy when you're in your twenties to feel like you're almost there, when really, you're only beginning.

But in addition to my Dream, I had a boy, a tall, cute one from Poland who had landed an internship at a software company in Milwaukee. A company that seemed likely to offer a job after he completed his internship. *Milwaukee?* part of me whispered. *But that's so close to home.*

Milwaukee? an equally sized part whispered. *Hooray! That's so close to home!*

But never mind that boy, never mind those plans: I would interview to become a missionary, just to be nice, and then go out to

New York and be a writing rock star, and maybe once I was *really* rich and famous, I'd write a book about Jesus for people.

But when I got to that interview, pencil skirt ironed, I was surprised that I knew the interviewer. He was someone who'd been to our campus to visit the missionaries before. He was smart and funny, and I really liked talking to him. He put down the sheet of questions, muttered, "These are kind of stupid," and asked me instead why I didn't want to be a missionary.

"Well," I said, "I guess because I don't just want to, like, work in ministry forever."

"Great," he told me. "I don't want you to either." Mission life, he told me, was more of a foundation for life after the mission. It was a place to prepare for going out into the big ol' Real World and being a fully formed Catholic. We need fully formed journalists, he told me, just like we need fully formed doctors and fully formed teachers and fully formed secretaries and, yes, fully formed ministry workers. Mission life, he told me, would help me be a better wife or mom or journalist or author or all of the above.

I went to Mass shortly after I was offered a job as a missionary and knelt, telling Jesus I was going to lay it all out on the table.

Here's my dream life, I told him, and that's when I realized: my #DreamLife wasn't my *dream life* at all.

My real dream life involved a house. A big one, with a wraparound back porch, a hammock, and plushy chairs that look like they're from Crate and Barrel but were probably bought on clearance at Target. A margarita, because I don't love liquor, and when I do drink, it's tequila. An open laptop with my very own story being written. Looking out across my giant backyard to see a trampoline with my husband and a gaggle of kids jumping and shrieking, all on a summer evening with fireflies and a light breeze. And a dog, lying by my feet, keeping watch over us all.

That's my dream life, I told Jesus, a bit surprised myself. *Not New York, and not being a FOCUS missionary. Just that. That simplicity and joy, that purpose and meaning.*

I am going to get you there, I felt him say to my heart, as clear as any words that have ever been spoken to me. *But listen: I'm using FOCUS to do it. Okay? You trust me?*

When Jesus asked Peter to walk out on the water, Peter was terrified. A human being walk on water? Jesus is standing there, his arm outstretched, and it all just seems so impossible. But there he is, asking Peter to walk, telling his friend to trust him. Jesus held out his hand, and when Peter trusted, he walked smoothly. It's only when he thought something like, *What the hell am I doing?* that he started to stumble (Mt 14:22–33).

And only a short time later, Jesus has risen from the dead and telling Peter the Denier that soon, Peter will have to go where he does not want to go (Jn 21:15–19).

He may have been speaking of New Orleans.

That's where I was sent, when I reached out my hand to clasp Jesus' and dove into that icy cold water. To New Orleans: home of crawfish and Cajuns, Mardi Gras and Mary statues. All I knew about New Orleans came from *The Princess and the Frog*. Sure, it looked fun, but . . . Louisiana? I am not a Southern girl. I'm Midwestern to a fault. I will be very polite upon meeting you, but if you don't know me and you try to hug me, I will cringe. I own a very, very warm coat. I say "bag" funny. I do Packers, not parades. Kringle, not king cake.

New Orleans was radically different from everything I knew in a thousand ways. It was not my dream life in any sense of the phrase: from the weather—unbearably humid in a way that gave me the first acne problems I'd ever had—to the way people spoke, flinging about French words and draping their sentences with a Southern drawl the same way Spanish moss hung from the oak trees. It was loud and bright, glitzy and gritty, serving pancakes sizzled in bacon grease and spicy jambalaya that made your eyes swell with tears. I was with teammates from the South who seemed *very* Catholic, who looked at me a little strangely when I used the word *feminism*, and who knew things like the name of Mary's mother and the gifts of the Holy Spirit. Who were so steeped in Catholicism that they didn't have to bring up the Chaplet of Divine Mercy on their phones when we prayed it.

The very culture of New Orleans was different than what I was used to. I remember being straight up *scandalized* to see a Confederate flag hanging off of someone's truck. Of course, the Midwest has its fair share of racial strife and a history of privilege as painful as any Southern city, but it doesn't sit so near the surface.

And hard things happened that year. A long-distance relationship is not an easy thing. The apartment I shared with my teammates was one small step up from what people might call a slum. I hadn't quite unclenched my fists from the idea that Working Hard = Saving Souls, and I was very determined to be The Very Best Missionary Ever. That meant early mornings and late nights, conversations I was determined to Get Right that didn't have a right answer and were far from black and white. I wanted an A+ on the nonexistent missionary report card. I was exhausted from constantly going, going, going, and I had no energy for investing in friendships with the large, fun group of Catholic young adults that lived in New Orleans. The students I worked with had good hearts, but many of them were so far from what I considered to be Catholic (which is, now that I think about it, what my teammates may have been thinking about me), as if being a good Catholic were something you could walk toward on a road map. They were complex and casual and, well, Cajun, with a culture I didn't understand and French words that I couldn't parse peppering their conversation. I had a difficult time connecting with them the way I had connected so easily as a student with the FOCUS missionaries on my own campus, and it made me feel like I was just constantly sabotaging our mission.

I felt lost, is what I'm saying. I had an image of missionary life, and what it actually turned out to be was a lot of lessons and a lot more gray than black and white.

But here is the very best thing about our Catholic Church: its universality.

I constantly turned back to the gospel verse of Jesus telling Peter to walk out onto the water. When Peter finally does step out, he suddenly panics; he starts to flounder, and that's when he begins to sink. It's in those moments when we realize what we're doing and panic.

For me, that panic looked like, *Wait a second. After earning a college degree, I took a job where I have to fundraise my own salary, and instead of spending my days drafting press releases to send to major outlets, I'm talking to an eighteen-year-old about why she needs to go to Mass on Sundays. What on earth am I doing?*

And then Jesus reaches out his hand and catches Peter. Jesus admonishes him a bit, calling him "of little faith," but that first part, the part where he catches him? That's what I cling to.

If we stay focused and keep our eyes on Jesus and walk steadily, we can do it. We can walk on water. We can walk on the path Jesus has claimed for us. When—not if—we panic and flail, crashing endlessly into the water, *he will catch us.*

So much of that year for me was flailing. I look back and want to give that Claire a hug. The one who thought mission was one big game that she could force a high score out of like Aaron Rodgers. The world needed missionaries, I thought, and the college campus was just fraught with sin and destruction. The fact that literally less than a year ago I was still struggling to attend Mass every Sunday and thought adoration was kind of weird meant nothing to me. I had Arrived at holiness, and damn it, I was bringing those Tulane University students with me.

And so often as I worked, I didn't keep my eye on Jesus. There were plenty of weeks where my goal had nothing to do with helping people meet the risen Lord and a whole lot to do with having 100 percent Bible-study attendance to impress my team director. I was rooted in success, not Jesus.

I let my own stupid pride uproot me, and that left me feeling as if I were drowning. But when Jesus reached out a hand to grab me, I preferred to wave him off and say, "I'm good." I was rooted to nothing—just flailing, like Peter.

The next year, I was sent to the University of Missouri. I had a parking spot, y'all. There was a Catholic center with organized retreats and a coffee maker. It was a whole different ball game. And although there, too, I felt the same internalized pressure to perform, something was different. New Orleans, in all of its heat and humidity and holiness, had changed me. That year of flailing had reminded me that mission is mission, whether there's a fancy office in your Catholic center or no center at all, whether your students are daily Mass goers or people who try to convince you Jesus was actually married. We are all seeking to know and be known, whether we live in Columbia, Missouri; or New Orleans, Louisiana; or Brookfield, Wisconsin. We are all on mission, and we are all being led.

Fast forward, like, six years. I'm no longer a FOCUS missionary, and I'm instead running *The Catholic Feminist* podcast. This little art project, this side hustle of mine, turned into a booming business. Strangers wanted to pay me money to talk about their products to my audience. Fans of the show did not appreciate this and would also like better audio quality, please. Listeners did not appreciate my casual cussing. People wanted to hear more about natural family planning because nobody's talking about it, but could we hear less about natural family planning because not all women are mothers? Strangers were sharing pictures of my kids online and sending me hate mail. It's still all very strange. But even though the feedback I receive is so much harsher than it was in FOCUS (I mean, Tulane students disagreed with me, but I was never once treated less than kindly or told I was sending souls to hell), I am really, truly, so much less anxious about it.

That's because I'm something *now* that I wasn't in New Orleans: I'm rooted.

It is my prayer with every podcast episode that I stay rooted in what matters. And I know, in my heart and soul, that what matters is not download numbers or what caliber of guests I can have on the show or how many advertising dollars we bring in or speaking gigs I'm offered or even, to be honest, how many books I write—those types of concrete markers of success that I wanted to point to as a missionary in New Orleans. What matters is that the show is moving people closer to the Gospel. Period.

In some ways, this is simply a change in spiritual maturity. If you're new to the faith (and you can be baptized as an infant and yet be new to the faith at fifty-seven years old, for the record), you're likely going to have a lot of work to do in your relationship with Jesus. I know I did. But I also see some concrete changes I've made.

The first is a solid change in attitude. Anthony Bourdain, a famous chef and food writer, was someone I followed closely and felt a connection with. He spoke at SXSW in 2016 and said something that greatly influenced my entire attitude toward the podcast and, to be honest, my career as a whole. He described having an attitude where he didn't really care how business went as long as he was authentic. He talked about walking into meetings with television executives and very much having an attitude of "I'll go back to brunch."[1] He may have had a choice word or two in there. But his point was, he was a famous food writer with multiple memoirs and television shows, but if everyone suddenly decided they hated him, he still had a skill set he could turn to. He'd just go back to making brunch, and he'd be fine. It allowed him to take risks and challenge people, to try things in new ways, to buck the rules and systems. Because he'd just go back to brunch if it failed, and he didn't care. This was my attitude with the podcast: I'll just go back to Barnes & Noble, where I worked in high school. I don't care if I lose every single listener and sponsor. If I have to work book retail for the rest of my life, I'll be fine. I'll just go back to brunch. Nobody's going to die. My family isn't going to be on the street. Every single person I know isn't going to wind up in hell if I have an off day (this sounds insane, but this is honestly the way my brain works occasionally). Why? Because my life is rooted in in the true vine of Christ, not in worldly achievements, and so long as the podcast reflects where I'm rooted, how people respond to it or to me doesn't matter.

The second change I made was being able to uproot ideas that were harming me. You need to weed the garden regularly in order for good things to grow. For us, those weeds are ideas that cling to us like moths to a flame, but the ideas are harmful and need to die. Maybe it's the idea that people are either good or evil, that there aren't shades of gray or circumstances you don't know. Or the idea that if we work hard enough, Jesus may finally toss us a handful of grace and then wait anxiously for us to mess everything up. Spiritual wounds from purity culture, lies that blossom from abusive relationships, untrue or unkind thoughts about ourselves—we can't just rip these from the ground. We must make sure to uproot the very causes and pain points of these harmful ideas in order to ensure that they don't return later when we least expect them. For me, this was the idea that the harder I worked, the more the world loved me, and, therefore, the more Jesus loved me. I have no idea where that idea came from, but we're all fed ideas by society that are demeaning and harmful and untrue. Instead, I had to remind myself of my natural worth: a worth that can't be earned or taken. As Jesus told us in Matthew 10:29–31, "Are not two sparrows sold for a small coin? Yet not one of them falls to the ground without your Father's knowledge. Even all the hairs of your head are counted. So do not be afraid; you are worth more than many sparrows." I am worth more than many sparrows, even if I'm not a gold medalist or a *New York Times* bestseller or a mom who feeds her kids organic vegetables. And that's something I have to constantly remind myself of.

Now, can everyone embrace a sense of rootedness that permeates their entire life? We all need an income. We need jobs. When I was a missionary and fundraised for my salary, I still owed it to my mission partners to work hard. I'm not saying you should be difficult to work with or walk around with a chip on your shoulder because only spiritual results matter. We can't just completely ignore the tangible results of our work. It's good to strive to do well and to set your eye on the prize. If we as missionaries hadn't tracked things such as Bible-study attendance, it would've been hard to say if the things we were doing on campus were resonating or if we should have changed evangelization tactics. What I am saying is that if you truly feel connected to Jesus, you know that he'll always have your back. I don't know if I knew that in New Orleans. I still saw grace as something to earn. Now that I know it's freely given, it allows me to live much more radically, knowing I always have the Lord to fall back on. And book retail.

So *how* do we stay rooted and uproot what needs to go?

Something that sets Catholicism apart from other religions is our sacraments and the fact that we can't do them on our own. You can whisper a quick apology to Jesus, but you can't grant yourself absolution. You can care for the poor, but you can't turn bread into the literal Body of Christ (unless you're a priest, in which case, thank you for your service!). You can say you believe in Jesus, but you can't baptize yourself in the name of the Father, the Son, and the Holy Spirit.

We can't do Church on our own, and that's a *good* thing. I remember, back at Tulane, having a conversation with a freshman in the student center. She told me that she just didn't *feel* God in Church the way she did on a hike or out in nature. You can, of course, feel Christ in nature, in the wind in the trees and the sound of a stream. He made them, so of course he's in them. But you can't be with him with the intimacy of the Eucharist at a state park. And those sacraments, especially the Eucharist, are no small things, no optional add-ons. The grace from the sacraments is an essential cornerstone of our faith. Speaking of the Eucharist, the *Catechism* says, "Finally, by the Eucharistic celebration we already unite ourselves with the heavenly liturgy and anticipate eternal life, when God will be all in all. In brief, the Eucharist is the sum and summary of our faith: 'Our way of thinking is attuned to the Eucharist, and the Eucharist in turn confirms our way of thinking'" (*CCC*, 1326–1327).

In New Orleans, even as I flailed and flopped, the rules of team life forced me into a rootedness I will forever be grateful for. Daily Mass, daily adoration, and daily Rosaries were part of my life during that season in a way they likely never will be again. That season desperately called for an intense rootedness, one that could only be strengthened through the power of Christ and his Church. Those routines we talked about earlier? They're essential for remaining in the vine. If we aren't using these physical touchstones, it's easy to get distracted by the things of the world and lose sight of why we're trying to bloom.

But in addition to staying rooted to the Church, we need to stay connected to the larger vision for our life. For example, there are plenty of times that raising little kids wears on me. Kids can be backbreakingly difficult, whether it's sickness during pregnancy or the tumult of potty training or the endless tantrums beating down on my eardrums. But as much as I love my little kids, I didn't plan to have a large family just for these little-kid years. I planned for one so that hopefully, one day, we're all around a giant Thanksgiving table, passing the potatoes and being with each other in a life-giving way. I have three siblings, and my holidays with them and their spouses are truly some of the most enjoyable moments of my year. But I'm sure there were plenty of times growing up when my parents questioned their sanity for having four kids. Staying connected to that vision of future Thanksgivings gives me the power to move forward during hard days and harder seasons. A listener of the podcast, Rhoda Bevc from Richmond, Virginia, told me a similar story: that she tries to constantly keep the end goal in mind. Nothing else truly matters besides her children becoming saints, even when they exhaust her. Staying rooted in a goal like sainthood is enough to keep anyone on track.

Or take my sister-in-law, who's wrapping up medical school. It's been far from an easy journey in many ways. But one day she'll be a doctor. She believes this is God's call for her in life. By staying constantly reminded of that vision, she can take the difficult exams and put up with the strangely anti-religion classes.

It's easy to blame social media, I think. We can point to the Big Bad Internet as the source of our struggles, but I don't believe that's quite honest, either. Comparison definitely existed before Instagram did—it's just that now, most of us are addicted to it. Back in the day, we didn't *know* what the woman next door was doing every second of the day. So it was much harder to be shamed by her work promotion and Jesse tree. "Social media" seems like an easy cop-out, a catchall term for *comparison* and *greed* and, ultimately, *sin*, and while it's not the cause of these things, the truth is, it does facilitate all of them.

Samantha El-Azem is one of my local friends and a tireless youth minister. She told me that when she feels herself being pulled by worldly pressures, shutting off her phone is the most helpful thing she can do. Getting down on the floor to play LEGOs with her kids reminds her of her ultimate call: that of a mother who loves.

Is it easy to blame social media for our lack of roots? Yes. Is it the only reason we lack roots? No. But does it help to turn it off? Yes.

It's also essential to remember that roots take time to grow. They don't just spring out from us like lightning when we discern our goal or take a break from Instagram. Think of it as moving to a new area and taking your time: meeting people, planting seeds of fellowship, and breathing out the Word of God like a calm, flowing river. Not jumping in like a flash in the pan, the way I'm so often tempted to. Seeds need time to root, and if you try to grow them hurriedly or they're transferred too quickly, they'll bear no fruit.

Roots aren't about what we look like at this exact moment. They're about connecting us to a source. They're about giving us new life.

SOUL-CARE STEPS

* **Create a daily reminder.** This can be as small as an image of Jesus taped to your bathroom mirror, but find something that's going to constantly remind you of your true purpose throughout the day.
* **Embrace the sacraments.** Staying constantly connected to Jesus through the sacraments of the Church is one of the best ways our Church helps us stay rooted to Christ. These are the things that help our roots grow down and really implant into the soil of Jesus.
* **Dream.** We want to live in the reality of our current day, and we should. But it also doesn't hurt to daydream a bit as a way to remind yourself what you're working for. So maybe you're breaking your back at a second job in order to earn money for an adoption. What will your future child's room look like? Start a Pinterest board and look at it when you need a reminder before you drive to that crappy work shift. Or pick out that farmhouse table online that you're going to buy for your huge Thanksgiving meals when all of your kids are a bit older. These dreams can help turn our struggles into a reminder of what we're working for.

6.
Planting Fellowship

I'm a firm believer that one of the most powerful places in your home is the table.

There have been seasons in my life when the table was a Craigslist coffee table, a folded card table, or no table at all. A breakfast bar, a dorm-eatery booth, a hand-me-down from my parents—these have all been the table at some point. The table where meals were held and fellowship was planted.

When I think of my own family, the family I grew up in, I think of life around the table. For many years, there weren't many dinners had there: someone had cross-country practice, someone had play rehearsal, someone had piano lessons. I was a child of the '90s, and while I feel like it's kind of in style these days to talk about growing up eating all *real food* and being *health oriented* and stuff, let me just say this: I definitely knew where the Swiss cake rolls were in the grocery store, and I remember eating Lucky Charms for dinner and feeling great about that decision. We were all-American in a way that very much included trans fats.

These days, when we're all back in Madison at my parents' house, the table is still where we tend to gather. Chips are poured (into bowls, because as my mother once told me as I dug my hand straight into the bag, "We are not *animals*"), and dip is spooned out. My kids and their cousin will be digging in the pantry for applesauce pouches. I know that my brother will eat all of the sour cream and onion chips and my sister will bust out the Oreos. I know my dad will insist he doesn't want anything but will steal pinches off everyone's plates. I know that right as we feel like we're about to go to bed, my mom will whip out more chips and we'll all have a few more handfuls, and my other brother will go to the fridge and put barbeque sauce on something it really shouldn't go on. I know my sister-in-law will drink white wine and that if you dare to venture to the fridge without offering to grab everyone else a beer, there will be hell to pay, as my husband can tell you from experience.

The table is the foundation for conversations, both easy and difficult. The most challenging of discussions are made a bit easier when someone's munching a s'more. That's how it is in my family and, probably, yours.

So why, when it comes to finding community, are we so afraid to open our damn doors and invite people to our table?

As the founder of *The Catholic Feminist* podcast, I get a lot of emails, emails about recent episodes or book recommendations. But I think the number one thing I'm asked is how to find community, as if community is something you find by looking hard enough and not something you build one awkward invitation at a time.

I'm as introverted as they get. Truly. I may come across as outgoing on the podcast, but it's a complete lie. There is nothing I love more than a really great library book, a cold glass of Pinot Grigio, and literally nobody within ten feet of me. The kindest thing my husband does for me is occasionally take the kids to the library on Saturday mornings. There's something about being alone in my house that gives me a sense of deep, real joy. Walking into huge parties makes me itchy. Really, that uncomfortableness with parties is why I can podcast—because if I'm having a conversation with someone, I want it to get to the meat of things and skip the small talk. I also want it to be one-on-one, not some big group to-do.

I think that sometimes we as introverts think we don't need community or that we can flourish on our own. As if a love for solo downtime and a need for other people are mutually exclusive. But that couldn't be farther from the truth. Being introverted just means that being with other people drains you and that you can only properly reenergize when you're alone. Introverts, who are probably more likely to pick a night in versus a night out, are the people who need community the most. We're the ones who will curl in on ourselves in times of trouble, the ones who will be slow to reach out in need. Extroverts run rushing headfirst into community; introverts wave a hand and say, "Nah, I'm good." That's why we need a solid group of people around us who can say, "No, you're not."

We as Christian people—both introverts and extroverts—were created to be in community with one another. Jesus was part of a community; when he went out and spoke, people said things like, "Hey, isn't that Jesus from Nazareth? Isn't Mary his mom?" He went and visited communities, eating at the tables of people he met. St. Paul focused on forming Christian communities so that people had accountability long after he left. Community—being with people who believe the same things you do, people who you can eat with and argue with and celebrate with—is the bedrock of human society.

"To be part of a Christian community is to belong to a group of believers who shun selfishness and give witness to God's love by loving and caring for one another," Pope Francis has said.[1] By being part of a community, we're given natural opportunities to shun the selfishness that lives in all of us. Cooking for someone else and taking the time to clean up after them is a concrete way to leave selfishness in the dust and care about your literal neighbor.

Similarly, the *Catechism* states that "the human person needs to live in society. Society is not for him an extraneous addition but a requirement of his nature. Through the exchange with others, mutual service and dialogue with his brethren, man develops his potential; he thus responds to his vocation" (*CCC*, 1879). By developing our potential, we're able to better serve in our vocation. Most of us are members of some form of community long before we enter religious life or get married or take a vow of singleness. Even something as simple as living in a sorority house can help prepare you to live in a house of religious sisters or a house full of kids. Have you ever met someone and just thought to yourself, *How do they function in society with other people? They seem so socially clueless.* They probably weren't part of a really solid community.

We've talked about how beautiful and important the universality of the Church is, and here is yet another way: we don't do Church by ourselves. We don't leave finding Jesus up to each individual. We come together and support one another, giving without expecting anything in return. The Church is a body made up of members.

But how many of these members do you know the names of?

How many of them have you not just socialized with, but truly fellowshipped with?

How many of them know your heart?

If your answer is zero or close to it, don't panic. You're not alone. I think most of us view Church as a sort of sacraments ATM. A place where you can check off your weekly Eucharist to-do or, better yet, where you can grow closer to Jesus, but not necessarily a place of community gathering. Not your *network*. Not your *people*.

We've formalized Church to the point of cringe. It can feel like if you want to make yourself more a part of a Church community, you're supposed to create a formalized event, a very specific roster of People Who Are Free Wednesdays at Six for Bible Study. Listen: sometimes that works. You've got to start somewhere. But you could also, I don't know, just say hi to the people who always sit behind you at Mass and ask their names. You could get the number of someone you always volunteer with in an awkward hi-I-need-friends way. You could set up playdates with other kids from your kids' school as a way to get to know their parents. You could ask one of the moms in your moms group if she wants to go to the zoo on Tuesday. You can chat with the woman who also practically lives at your favorite coffee shop. Yes, it's kind of uncomfortable, especially if you get rejected. But in the world of hashtags and Facebook groups and Twitter threads, it's like we've forgotten *how to make friends*. We've forgotten how to just talk to other people and try to form bonds with them.

Sister, you may need to go *first*, is what I'm saying here.

Going first looks like being the one to ask if someone wants to come over and watch the football game or celebrate a kid's birthday together. It is slightly terrifying, especially for us introverts, and I get that. Right after I had my first baby, I found myself in a season of loneliness, which is one of the worst seasons a person can go through. The devil loves loneliness. He wants us isolated and feeling like we have nobody to talk to. I distinctly remember walking around the park, pushing Benjamin in a stroller, and seeing moms happily chat while fat babies sat in swings. I wished for that *so* badly.

I could have just kept wishing. I could have made friends on the internet, which can be life-giving but can't quench the need for in-person interactions. Instead, I awkwardly went first. To a woman in church, to a friend of a friend who had kids, to a girl at the library. I invited people in—to my circle, to my home. I extended invitations and even made a goal of hanging out with one new person a month so that I could get to know more people in our suburb. And let me add that my home, at the time, was an apartment. A small, dark apartment with a *very* old couch and a coffee table we bought at a garage sale. One of the first couples we invited over later invited us to their home, which was a stunning Tudor with a fireplace straight out of *Fixer Upper* and a custom dining room table. The contrast was, shall we say, very good for my pride.

This online world we live in has positives and negatives. Certainly, true and meaningful connection can come from Instagram. If you've read someone's blog for years, sure, a part of you may feel like you know them. But it's no substitute for someone else's kid spilling milk on you or delivering a home-cooked meal to a friend who's just had a miscarriage. I think we've begun to be so plugged-in that we no longer feel like it's important to know our neighbors. But if we don't know the person next door has arthritis, how will we know that we should be helping them shovel their driveway? If we don't know the woman down the street has had horrible morning sickness with each pregnancy, how will we know she could really use someone to take her older kids off her hands once in a while? Getting close to people allows us to serve them so much better. We need to have these real-life friends, and we need to be in community with them.

I'm going to suggest you start with food.

Why? Well, for starters, we all need to eat. Jesus himself was hungry, asking for things to eat after he was resurrected (Jn 21:11–25), reminding us constantly to feed the hungry (Mt 25:31–46), and multiplying bread so that the crowds following him could have dinner (Mt 14:13–21). He knew hunger was a real, physical problem, and one that humans can only solve by feeding one another.

Secondly, food gives us something to *do*, so if things go horribly awkward, at least you can all talk about the chicken. (Part of going first means knowing that you may occasionally have a dud. Not everyone is going to click with you, and that's fine. I've hung out with people once and then they've slid off my radar because the friendship just didn't work out.) But most importantly, we start with food because food tells people who we are. It communicates some of our history and our values. It binds us together, doing this physical thing we all have to do to survive, this thing that can be such a great joy.

But stop. Look around your home right now.

Let me tell you what mine looks like: there are scratches in our hardwood floor—I'm not sure where they came from, but likely they're from a toddler's lawn mower being pushed across it. My kitchen counter is holding a few random empty paper bags and more than its fair share of peanut butter streaks. Our stovetop has a broken burner. My husband has a semi-annoying habit of leaving important papers stacked in the corner of the breakfast bar for weeks. Our kitchen table is tiny; it's from IKEA, but it fits in our kitchen. Our kitchen-table chairs are hand-me-downs from my parents, and they're old, as in, they're the ones we had when I was growing up. I'm not in the bathroom right now, but if I were to walk in there, there would probably be a towel on the floor and toothpaste on the sink. We could really use another chair in the living room, but I haven't gotten around to finding one I like, and the carpet I painstakingly picked off Wayfair has a teensy beer stain that you can't really see if you aren't looking for it. A blanket that doesn't match our living-room décor at all is draped across yet another hand-me-down couch.

But here's what you could see: a home. A home that's lived in because, hello, *people live here*. A family that would rather spend a weekend going on an adventure together than shopping for chairs. A stove with three brilliantly working burners. Joyful children (well, sometimes) pushing lawn mowers. A cozy blanket, because we like to be comfortable. A home that has seen tears and laughter, cheese and wine, hugs and hellos and goodbyes. A home where strangers are always welcome. And a pantry full of food.

When we bought our house, we did so specifically knowing that we love to open our door. We thought of that as we admired the open floor plan, as we checked out the size of the pantries. It brings us joy to have our friends and family over, to throw the door open and wave in people who need a hot coffee and a good venting session. Our basement is finished, meaning we can basically lock the kids down there with snacks and a billion toys, and we can pour the wine and have fellowship.

Fellowship is something deeper than socialization. It's building real relationships and seeing Christ in one another. It may start with talking about *The Bachelor* or football. But it's deeper than that: it means becoming true sisters and brothers in the Christian sense of the words.

When I was a missionary, a phrase thrown out a lot was "Acts 2 Church." "Acts 2" refers to scripture, where we hear about the creation of the early church:

> All the believers devoted themselves to the apostles' teaching, and to fellowship, and to sharing in meals (including the Lord's Supper), and to prayer. A deep sense of awe came over them all, and the apostles performed many miraculous signs and wonders. And all the believers met together in one place and shared everything they had. They sold their property and shared the money with those in need. They worshiped together at the Temple each day, met in homes for the Lord's Supper, and shared their meals with great joy and generosity—all the while praising God and enjoying the goodwill of all the people. And each day the Lord added to their fellowship those who were being saved (Acts 2:42–47, NLT).

So Acts 2 Church isn't Mass (and, therefore, doesn't replace Mass); it's a gathering: a gathering of believers together, to share meals with great joy and generosity while praising God.

So here, in our little brick house with scratched wood floors, we have some Acts 2 Church. And it is so, so eternally *life-giving*. To have fellow believers in your home, to serve them food made of your hands, is a way of acknowledging our shared humanity and sharing a bit of who we are with people. Food can heal divisions, it can soothe arguments, it can make bitter truths go down a bit sweeter. I can talk to people I disagree with over my grandma's pumpkin pie. I can make new friends over my mom's bacon-wrapped water chestnuts. I can share small pieces of my own heritage and history, delicious pieces that let the other person know that I want them to feel welcome, satiated, and full in my home and in my life.

When we traveled to Poland to visit Krzys's family, I was blown away not just by the taste of the amazing food but also by the sheer level of hospitality constantly offered. We'd eat and eat and eat; his grandfather even jokingly showed me how to push food further down in my stomach. His parents had warned me about six-course dinners, but I didn't really understand until I was handed course after course: different types of soup followed by delicious meats followed by savory pastries for dessert. The wine never stopped and neither did the pierogi or the conversation. And as I consumed this meal, it was so clear that it wasn't just made with delightful technical skill. It was made with love. It was the way Krzys's grandma made apple pancakes and talked about how much Krzys loved them when he was younger—they had this important memory together, shared over food.

Krzys and I like to joke that nobody should ever leave our house hungry or thirsty. We don't have a huge home, we don't have immaculate bathrooms, and most of the time we don't even have very well-behaved kids. But we do have wine and garlic and goat cheese, appetizers, and plate upon plate of dessert. I inherited the trait of always making way too much food from my mom, who I think has nightmares about people having to scrape the bottom of the Crock-Pot.

Here's what brings me joy: the smell of garlic and onions sizzling in olive oil, the feel of a freshly poured glass of Pinot Grigio in my hand, and the doorbell ringing. Friends entering, clutching bottles of wine. Friends we know well, friends we just met, but friends all the same. They're handed wine, coats are taken, children are banished downstairs (or, "Fine, you can stay up here, but no, you can't have a cookie yet, and please stop screaming about the latest episode of *Paw Patrol*"), and we have us some good ol' fashioned Acts 2 Church.

I would like you right now to weed out some of these thoughts from your brain:

My house looks nothing like Joanna Gaines's.
I don't know how to cook Real Food.
I'm a boring host.
I don't have enough money to feed other people.
I'm not great at starting conversations.
I don't own a serving bowl.
My kids warp into demons as soon as someone's looking.

To invite someone into your own dwelling is one of the most vulnerable things a person can do. I see it as a big old *yes* to God: "Yes, I'm an introvert, but I desire to know the people you have created and placed in my life. I desire to help them feel full, metaphorically and literally. I desire to feed them with your word and with Trader Joe's desserts." This isn't about recipes or table settings, although I do love both of those things. This is about relationships. Relationships that may need time to develop, the same way a roux needs time and constant stirring to thicken.

Here's what I want you to do: pick a family, any family. A family that looks like yours or a family that doesn't. The lonely looking young adult in your parish, the family with the five rambunctious children, the elderly couple you always sit behind, or the single mom at playgroup about whom you've always thought, *I feel like we would be friends.* The neighbors! *Whomever.* Someone who isn't already your best friend or related to you in some way. I want you to invite them into your home. I want you to cook them a meal. And when you eat it, I want you to think of God. The way Christ feeds us an eternal bread, and the way he satiates our deepest hungers. God, who did not *have* to create things such as gnocchi and jalapeño peppers and chocolate ganache but did because he loves us. You can have a sacred meal right there on your IKEA table with strangers who are now friends.

We cannot thrive without fellowship, without Christian brothers and sisters with whom we can say, *I'm there, too.* Jesus said that people would recognize us as Christians by the way we love one another (Jn 13:35). Think of your own community: Would people recognize you as a Christian by the way you love them? Or do you not know your neighbor's name?

I think a hallmark of a thriving person is one who knows he or she is loved. It's incredibly hard to thrive if you feel lonely and unsure of who's in your corner. Part of blooming is reaching toward the sun, saying, *Here I am. I need to be nourished.* The same way sunflowers reach for the sun, we can reach out to people for the nourishment we need.

I know the feeling of loneliness, and I know many of you do as well. What I *don't* think enough people know is the power of sharing a meal. Setting the scene for an experience of fellowship will move you closer to who you are meant to be, even if you're terrified, your baseboards aren't clean, and you're serving sauce from a can. It's *fine*, you guys. Nobody's going to die if something gets a little charred. A friendship will not be ruined because you forgot to put toilet paper in the guest bathroom.

You do not need a book to guide your discussion, and things don't need to be so formal. I was recently talking to a friend who works in ministry, and she told me the real goal of her job is just to get people connected so that they can then go out and do real, authentic ministry in their own homes.

"Maybe you don't need a knitting club through your parish, you know?" she said. "Maybe you just need to meet more people, and if a bunch of you like to knit, you're like, hey, let's knit at my house this Tuesday with some muffins. It doesn't have to be a whole *thing*. You don't need a *flyer* for it."

I also talked to a priest I know who told me something similar. What are the two most helpful things parishioners can do, he said? Pray for their priest and form real, authentic connections in their communities. That's it. Even if people don't volunteer to read or volunteer for children's liturgy or serve as a Baptism prep couple (all good things!), it is still so, so helpful if they try to make friends.

But it doesn't just have to be in your home that food is shared. As Shauna Niequist writes, "Food is a language of care, the thing we do when traditional language fails."[2] Think of how often we use food to show the people in our lives we love them, care about them, or want to get to know them better. We ask coworkers to lunch. We bring steaming casseroles to friends going through chemotherapy. We invite priests to our family picnics, cracking open beers and letting them not minister for a few hours. We bring food for new babies, and we bring food to funerals. We bake treats for children's birthdays, and in fact, for many of us, our first time truly feeding others was getting to pick that birthday treat. How amazing did it feel to walk into your elementary school classroom clutching your birthday cupcakes, knowing that everyone was going to eat in celebration of you?

Even the people you interact with every day can have better experiences when paired with the right food. Krzys and I don't go on dates nearly as much as we'd like because *children*. We could spend every day of our lives eating cereal for breakfast, sandwiches for lunch, and some kind of Crock-Pot meal for dinner. But what we truly enjoy is trying new food together. Some of our greatest dates have been date nights in with what we call "fancy snacks": something that's a step up from a bag of chips. Food elevates experiences; when we're trying new foods together and exploring different cuisines, we're stepping into the unknown as a pair. If my kids are having a hard day, I know a surefire way to bring us all together and get everyone laughing is to start doing make-your-own pizzas or surprise them with Nutella. When I'm having dear friends over that I know well, I still want to feed them well and try new things together. I love cooking my grandma's goulash as well as new things I found on Pinterest. Maybe you love making grilled cheese sandwiches or throwing frozen fries on a tray in the oven. Find what works for you.

I hosted Thanksgiving in 2019, and it felt like a personal challenge to make the perfect sweet potato casserole and stuff a turkey with rosemary and apples. I was excited to take the reins from my mom in a new way and cook the things I'd been eating for so many years. But the one goal I really had, deep in my soul, was to make my grandmother's pumpkin pie, complete with a homemade crust. Sure, I could have snagged a crust from the grocery store (and lest you think I'm Miss Bobby Flay, I bought frozen rolls, okay?). But this crust was my mountain to climb. My metaphorical crumbly

Everest. I practiced it beforehand and failed epically—too dry, too crumbly, too blech. In fact, I'm sort of notoriously bad at pies or at anything that requires patience. My mom offered to come over and walk me through it, because the truth is, although I *had* a recipe, the real way to make this pie is through feeling. It's to make it over and over again, with your mother. It's to roll the crust until it *feels right*, something you won't know until you do it a thousand times.

So I baked that pie alongside my mom, and it was like a piece of my grandma was with us, reminding us to add a little more water and not to over-flour the rolling pin. (I have a theory that my grandma purposely left out key parts of recipes so that nobody could ever bake as well as her. I'm sorry, but, "Add a little water"? "Bake the cookies until just before they're brown"? "Use good chocolate"? These are not instructions, Grandma. They're just not.) The first one? Total disaster. But by the time I'd made a few pies, I felt like I was finally getting the hang of things.

Having people over is the same way. You've got your recipe and you've cleaned your floors, but guess what? A kid's going to drop juice on your rug, and you're going to buy the wrong kind of potatoes for your recipe, and you're going to send your husband to the grocery store halfway through the evening because you're low on beer. Maybe you invited over an awkward couple who doesn't know how to keep a conversation going, or maybe you had to eat off paper plates. But you know what? You'll get the feeling ironed out. You just need to do it a few times. Keep trying. You'll get there. I didn't always love hosting, and I certainly didn't always love cooking, but I, like everyone, have always loved feeling seen and known. I've loved making other people feel full. I can't promise you many things, but I promise you that having a gaggle of people you like on your porch and pouring chips and salsa into bowls is not that hard. And the reward—that sweet sense of fellowship—is very, very worth it.

Food is a sensory experience that deepens our senses and reminds us of our humanity. But it's also one of the most concrete ways we can show love, and one of the most fulfilling ways we can receive it.

"You are loved," the poet Mary Karr wrote. "Take that and eat it."[3]

SOUL-CARE STEPS

* **Invite someone over.** Y'all, it's that simple. Building a community begins with extending an invitation for dinner. It can be spaghetti, it can be stew, it can be desserts and coffee, but make it involve food and make it at your home. Once you do it a few times, it gets easier.

* **Find a recipe that makes you feel good.** I don't just mean good in your body (although that's important too). I mean good in your soul. When I'm baking bread, I can't really explain it: I just feel like *me*. I love the smell of yeast, I love the practice of kneading, I love the way I can read a book while I wait for it to rise. I love working toward the perfect sourdough. I love the smell of crusty bread being pulled apart, waiting to be dipped in balsamic vinegar and covered in cheese. Find something you love to make—and I have some suggestions that my friends and I love in the appendix for you to try out—and then feed the people in your life with it.

* **Break bread.** I know, I know—asking you to have someone over for dinner feels like a mountain. But it's not, y'all. It's such a climbable molehill. Your bread may be pancakes after church or chili on a football Sunday. It may even be a bowl of Halloween candy. Break bread with new faces and see in them the face of Christ.

Part Four

Bursting into Bloom

GOD WANTS US TO BE HAPPY
ALWAYS. HE KNOWS US AND HE
LOVES US. IF WE ALLOW THE LOVE
OF CHRIST TO CHANGE OUR HEART,
THEN WE CAN CHANGE THE WORLD.
THIS IS THE SECRET OF AUTHENTIC
HAPPINESS.

—POPE BENEDICT XVI

7.
Happy for Now vs. Joy Eternal

I have a horrible habit that I'm trying to get rid of, but it's one that's somehow buried itself deep into my bones. I'll be somewhere amazing, doing something truly life-giving—maybe enjoying a drink with my husband at a beautiful restaurant, looking out across the frozen lake at my family's cabin, watching one of my kids master a skill they've been working on for ages, or tickling them and hearing their shrieks of joy—I'll be *in it*, in the moment, and then a thought will burst into my brain.

What about sex-trafficking victims?

Somewhere, there's a girl being trafficked. There's a girl who wants nothing more than to snuggle up with her mom and read a book. There's a girl who's starving, a girl who's being abused, a girl who's in the clenches of addiction: girls, girls everywhere, hurting and humiliated, broken and beaten. The suffering of those girls weighs so immensely on my shoulders, and it clouds my vision. Suddenly, the joy of seeing my two-year-old daughter's belly pop out from underneath her shirt is gone. The happiness I get from a long sip of hot coffee is ripped away. All I can think of is *suffering*—the suffering I haven't had to experience, the suffering I'm suddenly sure is waiting for me, or the suffering I'll have in hell because I *haven't* had intense suffering here on earth.

I'm suddenly in a mental tailspin, and while the friend I'm chatting with is telling me how much fun she had and how glad she was to be with me, I'm secretly thinking, *This was a waste of time, and we should be out raising money for new freshwater systems for Mexican refugee camps.* I have a hard time seeing joy or laughter or hope; instead, all I see are the ways in which we've failed the world.

I begin to feel like God doesn't want me to be happy. That it's not *fair* for me to be happy. That I should be weeping now, so that I can laugh later.

I mean, Jesus says it over and over again in the gospels, right? When he had everyone gathered on the mountain, he proclaimed, "Blessed are the poor in spirit, for theirs is the kingdom of heaven. Blessed are those who mourn, for they will be comforted" (Mt 5:3–4). But what about the times when I'm striving to *be* rich in spirit, *not* to be mourning?

I also recently read the *Diary of St. Faustina* last year, and the Polish nun writes in detail about having a vision where a group of people were merrily dancing along a path before they drop into the underworld of hell. Um . . . *yikes.* Followed of course by the thought, *Is that me? Am I dancing merrily along in life, just waltzing toward eternal damnation because I have a cute house and a KitchenAid mixer and can really get down on the dance floor at weddings?*[1]

So then I see a megachurch preacher, waving his arms around, yelling at us that we deserve all of the health and wealth the world has to offer. Or Kanye West, chuckling to James Cordon that he converted his heart to Jesus and then got a huge tax return in the mail.[2] I see those who pray for good parking spots and insist upon God hearing their prayers as they pull into the closest ones. The rich, the powerful, the strong, denying entry to those whom they deem less, insisting there isn't room at the table. Oppressing and ostracizing, usually in the name of money and happiness. And I think, *They will get their reward, and it ain't gonna be pretty.*

I also shudder at most self-help books, particularly a certain brand of self-help books for Christian women. They tend to give off advice that seems extremely unchristian to me. The advice of "putting yourself first" and "going after what you want above all else." Putting yourself first seems to be literally the *opposite* message of the Gospel. Sure, take your bubble bath and do your yoga, but putting your own needs in front of others' starts to feel a lot like that dysfunctional family we talked about in chapter 4, the one in which some members have more than enough while others have barely enough. If your own "needs" are causing your brother or sister to not have food to eat, surely our system of self-help has crumbled.

Surely God doesn't want us to be happy, right? He wants us to be "poor in spirit" and "brokenhearted"—those are the people that get to heaven. The rest of us suckers are pretty much doomed. How do we live in this tension? This tension of lifting up those who are mourning while not losing ourselves in our own desperate search for whatever we deem "happiness" to look like?

But.

Then you dig through the Bible a little closer, and different phrases pop out at you:

> "Those whom the LORD has ransomed will return and enter Zion singing, crowned with everlasting joy; They will meet with joy and gladness, sorrow and mourning will flee" (Is 51:11).

> "Restore to me the gladness of your salvation" (Ps 51:14).

> "I have told you this so that my joy may be in you and your joy may be complete" (Jn 15:11).

> "The humble will be filled with fresh joy from the LORD" (Is 29:19, NLT).

So, I'm sorry, but which is it, God? Do you want us wailing and gnashing our teeth, or filled with "fresh joy"?

If I'm not thriving, if in fact I feel like I'm barely *surviving*, is this God's will? Am I just supposed to be this unhappy? Does God even want happiness to be part of my thriving? Does he want me to cry myself to sleep every night over the weight of the world?

I think you know the answer to this last question: no.

This is what I'm finding: we have a complex God. Our God is not easily wrapped up in think pieces or homilies; he's not a Lord of hot takes or even books. God cannot be summed up in a podcast episode. He's a big God, a flowing God, a God that descends upon our hearts and wishes for us to know the *fullness* of life.

The fullness: the oil and the vinegar. The bitter and the sweet.

I do not believe that a God who created each of us in our own unique way desires us to be full of mourning and weeping. If it were God's plan for humanity that we all just be depressed all the time, he wouldn't have created goat cheese or library books or sunsets or pumpkin spice lattes. I think in the moments we love each other the strongest, God is there: in the whispered secrets and the prized conversations, in the comfort and the chaos. When we are joyful, we are living out the true song God has written for us.

So what is the key differentiator between joy and happiness? It's what those things are found in. Joy is found in the Good News of the Gospel: it's something that can't be stolen or squashed. Happiness, while certainly not a bad thing, is so much more temporary. A difficult day of work can, for me, make happiness hard to hold onto. Joy is deeper: it outlasts moments and moods; it's more a way of life than an emotion. Because nothing can take away the Good News. As Paul writes in Romans 8:38, "For I am convinced that neither death, nor life, nor angels, nor principalities, nor present things, nor future things, nor powers" can separate us from the love of God and, therefore, our source of joy.

When we are weeping: *Emmanuel, God with us.*

When we are filled with happiness: *Emmanuel, God with us.*

It's called the Good News for a reason, and we should live as if we know that Good News. St. Teresa of Avila is known to have begged God to save us from *gloomy saints*, and so we should try not to complain or be miserably pious but instead experience the fullest joy we can in order to show others that the Good News is real. That Jesus died and rose again. You're not holier if you mope or complain constantly or if you're the person in the room always pointing out how hard you (or even other people!) have it. This isn't a contest for who is more broken in spirit.

But part of living out this Gospel message is to serve others in abundant and radical ways. And in part, this does mean helping to carry the weight of their worries. We *should* be thinking of sex trafficking, is what I'm saying. But we shouldn't view it as a cloud that covers our entire life, one that prevents us from enjoying the good things God has given us.

Furthermore, it's always important to note that people in worse-off circumstances do not exist to make *you* feel better. I know we talked about this in chapter 4, but listen, sister. Here's a fresh cup of coffee with a few shakes of sugar. Those people you may think are barely getting by could quite possibly be living a more abundant life than you, one more full of joy and hope and song. My sister travels to Belize every year as part of a long-term missions project (not the type of missions where they wear matching shirts and paint a house, but the type where they provide financial support for new schools over many years, hiring local labor and celebrating in God's abundance together). She's told me over and over again about how little some of the people there have, in diet and finances and resources. But in her view, their joy seems to be insurmountably greater than what other people with greater resources generally have. They're *happy*. Of course, you don't want to paint people as caricatures—some people in the area she visits are probably crab apples or jerks or whatever. But for the most part, they have a sense of joy, not in what they have materially but in what they have *eternally*.

I do think God wants us to be happy. I think the Bible's written that way, in Psalms and Isaiah and John. I think much smarter people than me have said so, including St. John Paul II, who said that "people are made for happiness. Rightly, then, you thirst for happiness. Christ has the answer to this desire of yours. But he asks you to trust him."[3]

To trust in Jesus is not one decision we make suddenly, like we're standing on the top of a huge sledding hill clutching a chunk of plastic and decide to head down. It's a thousand miniscule decisions that make up our days, a constant fiat that can have really, really difficult real-world consequences. I spoke to a medical school student who had to bravely tell her rotation that she wasn't going to sit in on abortions, leading to consequences in her career. I've met friends who have moved across the country, quit their jobs, or adopted children, all in the name of *trusting Jesus*.

But what are we trusting him to *do*? That's the unspoken part of the question that so often remains unacknowledged. Because sometimes I think a small part of us is "trusting him" to make us *happy*, which isn't really what he promised. In fact, I think there's a lot in the gospels about how hard the road is going to be for Christians. I'm pretty sure he tells us we're going to have to go "where you do not want to go" (Jn 21:18) and that the world will hate us because it hates him (Jn 15:18–25). *Nowhere* in scripture does he promise that a life of trusting him and avoiding sin is going to lead to things such as financial prosperity or worldly accolades. If that were the case, we'd consider anyone who lives in Beverly Hills as an almost-saint and 90 percent of the world as total sinners who were reaping the rewards of a life lived without Jesus, and we all know *that's* not an accurate photo. Worldly success and holiness clearly do not correlate. It's part of why the prosperity gospel absolutely enrages me—it couldn't be more counter to the Gospel. So if it's not worldly success, what are we trusting Jesus to get us to?

A *complete joy*.

And that joy may not look like what we thought it would.

My #DreamLife, that one I had envisioned, did not come true. Hardly at all. Yes, I'm writing books and married to an interesting, generous, funny person. But I live in the Midwest, in a smaller-than-average house. I do not own a pencil skirt. I'd say my fame and fortune is pretty evenly divided between people who appreciate what I do and people who think I'm dragging souls into hell by using the word *feminism*.

Jesus is not an ATM, one where you put in Good Deeds and get a #DreamLife spat out. And thank God—literally—for that. Otherwise we'd all be living in agony. Because we're all plagued with sin and bad choices, roads taken that should have been avoided. And what if we had to constantly *earn* things like health and the ability to work to pay for rent and organic bell peppers? Those things are great. But Jesus does not dole them out to the well-behaved and withhold them from sinners.

So if you're waking up each day with a battle to fight, know this, sister: Jesus has a plan. Not for your *happiness*, but for your *joy*.

I think Jesus likes when we're happy. But I know this: I'm a mother of little kids. And so often they're mad at me. I mean, *often*, you guys. My son in particular is what we call a Runner. It is the dream of his life to be as far away from me in public at any given moment. He likes to hide, which is fine if we're home and he's hiding in one of his three regular spots in our very small house. But it's *not* fine in the public library, which is what happened the other week. I turned my back on him for one minute to help his little sister reach a book, and when I turned around, he was gone. Any mom knows the absolute terror that comes from not knowing where your kid is, even if it's just for a second or two. It is truly the most frightened I've ever been, with my heart pounding so loud I could feel it in every single body part. I called his name a few times and almost got teary when the young, calm librarian told me he'd just seen a toddler take off; was it mine? Did I need help? We looked around for not more than three minutes before he was found crouching behind a couch, giggling at his own misbehavior.

And he received the verbal ass-whooping of his little life. I explained to him, in a steady Mommy Is Very, Very, Very Angry with You Right Now voice, that he could hide in our house, because Mommy always knows who is in our house and knows the space very well. In a library, Mommy might not be able to find him, and that was very scary for Mommy, and listen, kid, you just gave me a heart attack, so please do not ask me how many books you can check out right now.

On the drive home, he told me in his powerful, squeaky little voice, that he was "very, very fwustewated" with me, because I was so mean and never let him do anything fun.

How often are we very, very fwustewated because we want to hide in the library, but that's *not* what will make us thrive?

The difference between me and Benjamin is practically nothing compared to the difference between me and God. And my frustrations with God have been much larger than whether or not I can hide in a library, but that doesn't make them any less real. I have sent many prayers filled with tears heavenward.

Jesus has plans we can't see. All we see is the joy of running, the thrill of hiding behind a couch. We don't see the way it's affecting the other people around us or the hurt and terror our plans may cause. Our view is so, so small. When we're trusting Jesus, we're trusting him to help us become saints, not trusting him to give us everything we've ever wanted. I think once again of New Orleans: a place where I so often didn't feel *happy* (although when I did, it usually involved some kind of fried dough). But I do think of that year as joyful. I was in the trenches, doing mission, praying and breaking bread with three teammates who loved the Lord desperately and inspired me daily. It's hard to explain unless you've been in a place where you've held both pain and joy in the same hand. You suddenly know the feeling of finding the risen Lord: hallelujah, he is here, but that doesn't mean the path is smooth. Ask St. Paul: the burden is light, but it might get you put in prison.

I think most of us know the feeling of chasing after something we were certain was going to bring us joy but simply didn't. Maybe it was a college: *once you get into that school, you'll be happy*. Maybe it was a vocation: *once you get accepted to religious life, you'll be happy*. Maybe it was a career milestone: *once you land a book deal, you'll be happy*. That was surely my attitude when it came to getting my novel published. And once it was purchased by a major publisher, I was surprised to find the Very Same Me waking up in bed the next morning and a whole new avalanche of stresses to be concerned with.

Those things are *good* things. We've all wanted bad things we were sure would make us happy because we know so much better than God. *If I could just find a different guy than the one I'm seeing, I'd be happy. If I just had one more drink, I'd be happy. If I could just tune out my kids asking things of me, I'd be happy.*

With both the good and bad things we insist will make us happy, we're hiding behind couches, chuckling while Jesus searches for us, so sure that *we* know what's best for us.

But if we're waiting to be happy until a certain moment clicks into place, think of all the things we're missing out on: the people we could be forming into disciples, the relationship that could become the bedrock of our vocation, the career that could teach us vital information for the future, or the community that may help us learn about an important social issue. These things could all pass us by because we're so focused on Someday. But while we're waiting for that #DreamLife, we can still make such a huge difference in God's kingdom here on earth.

It doesn't make any sense, the way we feel a surge of joy when we give something away, when we stand in solidarity with neighbors who don't look like us, or when we've interacted in a God-honoring way with someone who drives us crazy. The *joy* we feel when we confess our sins and receive absolution makes no sense either. You read those things and think you'd feel miserable after them. What we really want is not to suffer, for our lives to be as easy and pleasurable as possible, involving wine and laughter and little struggle. But life in the upside-down kingdom of God means that things aren't what they seem. You're joyful when you're radically giving and miserable when you're clinging onto your possessions for dear life.

I heard a podcast episode once where the host started talking about making a list of what really made him happy and then realized he spent his money in all the wrong places. He had a gorgeous mansion with an ocean view, but he didn't even like swimming or hanging out at the beach. His choices in life didn't reflect things that actually made him happy.

I thought about what really, truly gives me life, big and small: Coffee dates with dear friends who know my heart. Floating in Fishtrap Lake. The sound of my kids playing at the splash pad. Really great novels with hopeful endings. Cold, crisp wine. *The Great British Baking Show* marathons. Seeing movies in the theater with my husband.

Do my life choices reflect a sincere urge to take part in these experiences? Am I saying no to enough work events that I can actually make time to go on dates, or am I convinced that we desperately need one hundred more dollars? Am I leaving my phone at home when we go to the splash pad so I can be present, or am I focused on capturing the perfect angle for Instagram? Am I actually reaching out to those friends to get dates on the calendar so we can have some desperately needed one-on-one time, or am I just thinking about it without ever reaching out to them?

Much of life is out of our control and out of our grasp. But I think we forget that so much of life isn't. We forget that if we are desperately unhappy, we can make small changes that nudge us closer to true joy. Oftentimes, we reap what we sow, and if we're sowing bad decisions (or even just lazy ones) and things that bring us closer to worldly happiness and further from godly joy, that is precisely what we will reap.

Not me, you might be thinking. *I did not sow this.* And sister, maybe you didn't. Maybe you're in a situation that's completely out of your control. Maybe you sowed good seeds only to find a garden of weeds in return.

But here is the problem with relying on concrete, material things of this world to bring us happiness: they're so temporary. Life is temporary, your fancy new house is temporary, and your job is temporary. It will all wash away one day, and all that's left will be how we responded when the Lord called our names. The things making you happy today can be stolen from you tomorrow, in an instant, like so many of us know. Putting our happiness in the things of this world is only going to lead to *un*happiness, every time. In contrast, putting our hope in the eternal gives us that *complete* joy Jesus speaks of. Because yes, I'm happy when I'm drinking a margarita on the porch and I'm with people I love and the sun is beginning to set. But without God, that joy wouldn't be complete. It's the *Good News* that truly makes that experience enjoyable. Because I'm *thankful* for the gift of rest and the taste of tequila and the beauty of the weather, that I know what love is, and that I feel it for the people I'm with. By showing me what love is through the life of his Son, God makes that experience more complete, and he makes it one worth living.

So often what brings us happiness is tiny. Caryll Houselander writes in *The Reed of God* about this, saying, "A seed contains all the life and loveliness of the flower, but it contains it in a little hard black pip of a thing which even the glorious sun will not enliven unless it is buried under the earth."[4]

When we feel buried underneath the earth, when we have to wait before we can bloom, there is one person that decides if we are joyful. It is not our boss, our doctor, our mother-in-law, or our children. It is us.

This is a bitter pill to swallow, and I know that. My mom loves to drive me crazy by insisting, "Nobody can make you feel anything." And it took twenty-eight years, but I finally believe she may be right.

You decide to be sad.

You decide to be lonely.

You decide to be angry.

Sometimes these are good decisions, because they point us toward truth and action. I know that there have been times in my life where I've been deeply sad, and it brought me closer to God, allowing myself to feel that mourning and sit in that sadness. But sometimes we need to take a deep breath and nail those emotions to the Cross because they are not benefitting us or bringing God's kingdom to earth.

Here is the good news, the flip side of that coin: *you decide to be joyful.*

In one study, two psychologists decided to see the impact gratitude had on a person's overall well-being.[5] They asked a group of people to write about things they were grateful for each day, and they asked another group of people to write about the daily irritations they experienced. Unsurprisingly, those who expressed thanks for the things they'd experienced each day had a higher level of happiness and felt overall better about their lives. When we take time to reflect on what's around us—truly take time, not just a casual nod toward heaven here or there when we guiltily realize we haven't in a while—we begin to feel better about the life around us. Our joy begins to take root, and like any other plant, we water it. We talked earlier about the importance of gratitude in perspective and why gratitude helps us learn important truths around us. *Gratia*, the Latin root of the word *gratitude*, means grace. It's fitting, then, that when we give gratitude, we participate in grace—we become the receivers, accepting what God hands to us with a complete, full-fledged joy.

It took me a long time to make peace with uncertainty, to understand that God loves me. Not me the perfect writer, or me the mother who does arts and crafts, or me the sister who never forgets to call. Just me, entirely. Me wholly, the good and the bad.

I used to pray the way you ask someone to do something they really don't want to do: *please, please, please, and here's all the reasons why.* I thought Jesus hated my happiness and would only give it to me if I knocked hard enough, if I suffered long enough, if I begged with an adequate amount of groveling. Now my prayers sound more like the wind through the trees. They feel like an outstretched hand: I request, and now I am ready to accept joy in whatever form God gives it.

SOUL-CARE STEPS

★ **Do something small that brings you joy.** This is allowed to be shallow. In fact, I think it ought to be in order to remind yourself that God does not hate our shallow happiness, that he makes room for the small pleasures that put a smile on our face. Eat a really good cookie, savoring every bite. And let yourself *enjoy it*—don't suddenly panic about your eternal damnation.

★ **Do something small that brings someone else joy.** A phone call to an elderly relative you haven't spoken to in a while. A spontaneous trip to the grocery store to pick up some healthy donations for the food pantry. A small gift card for coffee emailed to someone in your life going through a hard time. To give joy is to get it. We can't let our joy stop with us.

★ **Give thanks.** Above all else, no matter our circumstances, we *should* have joy. Pause and give thanks to God for that Good News, and do something that will remind you to give thanks daily. Maybe it's a gratitude journal, maybe it's a daily Hail Mary, but find a way to practice gratitude daily.

8.
Embracing the Seasons

You know who don't fear death?

Gardeners.

They know that plants die—it's part of their cycle. Gardeners go out in the fall and tear up perennials, looking over at their cold, brown garden beds and having hope for the spring. They don't anxiously go out and buy new plants. They don't weep that their gardens have moved on. They embrace a new season—a season meant for quiet growth that isn't seen.

The past few years I've found myself feeling pulled to live as seasonally as possible. I've been reading novels that take place in the season I'm in—no snowy mysteries read in the summer or summer romances flipped through in the autumn. We've been trying to buy more local produce, meaning that our diet has gently shifted toward being more aligned with the seasons. Living seasonally reminds me of some sort of clichéd day of old: as the sun goes dark earlier and earlier, we want to sleep earlier and earlier. It's dark and cold, and we want to rest. In spring, we feel a pull toward new growth: new goals, cleaned-out closets, floors that smell of pine-scented Lysol, and new plans for the year ahead. And then, in the summer, we want to stay up until the last slice of sunlight has left the sky. We want to sip margaritas and splash our feet in pools, rubbing aloe on red skin and embracing the bounty. As we turn back toward fall, we want to sip hot drinks in front of classic television shows, feet buried under blankets as the air smells of smoke and Halloween candy.

God gave us four seasons. These days, you really don't need to live seasonally. You can crank the temperature in your home up or down as much as you want. Strawberries can be found in January and ordered to be dropped at your front door within two hours. We have electricity, meaning the light of the sun doesn't guide our days. Seasonal living is something that seems quaint and old-fashioned.

And sure, we're using our lights. We're not Luddites. But our family has also felt a powerful peace in embracing the seasons and living closer to the earth, letting God's divine plan for our world guide us in our way of life.

Just like our yard and the atmosphere go through seasons, so, I'm convinced, do our spirits. As Ecclesiastes reminds us, "There is an appointed time for everything, and a time for every affair under the heavens" (Eccl 3:1). There are seasons of growth and there are seasons of rest, and recognizing the difference between them is key to a healthy, thriving spiritual life.

SPRING

In a season of spiritual springtime, you feel a sense of growth. Maybe you've just found a priest whose podcast you're obsessed with, and it's leading you to all sorts of spiritual awakenings. You likely feel hopeful for what is to come—a hope in your spiritual knowledge and, much more powerfully, hopeful in the risen Lord. You probably recognize that overflowing feeling of hope because you want to tell *everyone* about the new thing you found that is helping your spiritual life grow. I have a friend here in Milwaukee who's so obsessed (and rightfully so) with *He Leadeth Me* by Fr. Walter Ciszek that the second I meet someone in the area who also is reading it, we both start laughing because obviously she's the one who told us to read it. More recently, I stumbled upon a podcast called *The Bible Binge* that talks about difficult-to-understand Bible stories as if they're pop-culture shows. It "casts" characters with actors and provides context for things I sometimes don't know, such as how big of a city Nazareth is or the standing shepherds had in society. It filled me with a desire to learn more about the Bible, plant seeds of knowledge within my heart, and dive into areas of scripture I'd previously stayed away from (hi, bye, Leviticus, and

I'm not sorry about the times I've skipped you in the past, because you're a whopper).

This sense of springtime can also be reflected in our material world. My last month or so of pregnancy often feels like springtime to me. I'm finally starting to get over the harshness of a hyperemesis winter, and I'm completely inspired by new growth and new literal birth. If you've just moved to a new area and are feeling hopeful about your new job, if you've just started a new medication that's promised to take away some of your chronic pain, or if your eyes have just been opened to the problem of homelessness in your area and you've drafted up a volunteer schedule with your local shelter, you may be feeling like your spirit is in a season of springtime.

Morgan Partlow, a graduate student at Missouri State, recently shared with me the story of her dad's passing. "Instead of falling away from my faith in the midst of grief and loss, I felt I had no choice but to lean into it," she explained. "When Easter rolled around, I felt my life was mimicking the world around me. The world was still dead and gray, but a little bit of green was starting to show. Pieces were starting to come back to life. Just as Jesus rose, I felt myself rising out of grief and into an entirely new and beautiful relationship with him. It took a truly terrible situation to make me realize I would never be in full bloom without surrendering myself and my life fully to Jesus."

During seasons of spring, it's important to constantly stay connected to the Lord. Just as we need to frequently water our plants after we embed them into the earth, we need to make sure our movement toward action is being properly guided. When we just grow, grow, grow without pausing to drink from the eternal waters, we may be walking into spaces we shouldn't be and yanking others around with us. Part of growing means taking time to listen.

SUMMER

Summer is my favorite season. In Wisconsin, our summers are stunning: fireflies and campfires, sunsets and slight breezes. I especially love summer up at my family's cabin, paddle boarding across the lake until my arms ache before jumping in the water to cool down. It sounds like ice clinking in a glass, fireworks exploding, dripping peaches being sliced open, and sunscreen being squeezed out of a faded green bottle.

When your spirit is in a season of summer, it's in a season of enjoyment. It's a joyful, exuberant pause: the seeds have been planted, but it's not yet time to harvest them. As the song says, "Summertime, and the livin' is easy."[1] You're feeling especially close to Jesus and have a deep sense of inner peace. When I think of a season of spiritual summer, I think of the sweet time right after my first child was born. He was an exceptionally easy baby; he slept through the night at seven weeks old and loved to just be held or sit in his bouncer, hanging out and looking out the window. That time reminds me of long walks around the neighborhood, sipping iced coffee and holding my husband's hand. Even though I was a new mom, I felt like a pretty good mom and like I could handle anything the world threw at me. It was joyful, pure and simple. I wasn't intensely learning, but instead just taking in whatever the day threw at me and enjoying it. It felt like true *rest*.

This is a sweet season that the Lord bestows on us and wants us to thrive in. When we're embracing summer, it's important to truly *embrace* it, not just wait for the other shoe to drop. The lack of schedule we may experience in the summer reminds us that we were born to be free from worldly standards, finding true joy and order only in our resurrected Christ. Because what if I had spent that summer worrying about my *next* child, whether she would be so much harder than my first one? (Spoiler alert: she was.) I would have lost those few weeks with my sweet boy, that precious time when babies want to curl up on your chest and take lengthy, dream-filled naps.

Katie Pyles, a youth minister in Elburn, Illinois, told me she felt like she was living a spiritual summer in high school. "I was part of a thriving youth ministry. It was joyful, beautiful, and safe," she said. Katie Kaczmarski, a digital product designer in Hyattsville, Maryland, also told me about a spiritual summer, but hers was radically different: teaching in rural Kenya, where she was able to be surrounded by the beauty of nature. My spiritual summer looked very different from Katie Pyles's and Katie Kaczmarski's, and yours will probably look different too. Don't compare, and don't wait for what's next. Instead, enjoy the summer, and embrace how God is showing you his love in this moment.

Isaiah may have been in a spiritual summer when he wrote, "Those whom the LORD has ransomed will return and enter Zion singing, crowned with everlasting joy; They will meet with joy and gladness, sorrow and mourning will flee" (Is 51:11).

FALL

Autumn is a time of harvest, of reaping the fruit you have planted. This can be good: gathering bounties of vegetables or, in our more modern cases, passing our dissertation defense or watching our child dance in her first recital or celebrating the woman you've been mentoring as she's accepted to law school. But it can also be more dreary: witnessing how our addictions have a serious impact on others or coming to a reckoning in marriage therapy or being let go from a job we weren't a good fit for. Maybe it feels like Jesus has pulled back a bit, and you're feeling loneliness settle in: a quiet loneliness, one that you sit with in front of a crackling fire, the eerie stillness of no longer feeling a peaceful joy.

Fall has often been reduced to an aesthetic in our society; it's Instagram images of pumpkin spice lattes and riding boots on leaves.

But fall is actually death.

My sister loves fall, as she will tell you in her gigantic hoodie, sipping coffee by a harvest-scented candle and streaming *Halloweentown*. But my mom has always disagreed, shaking her head.

"Fall is just death," she says. "Everything is dying."

And it's true—fall *is* death. Leaves change color, dropping from trees, and those trees shudder into a deep slumber. Plants turn into brown crinkles of mess, and birds flock south, loudly proclaiming that it's time to move on. The trees become barren, stark reminders of how little we have.

There may be something in us that needs to die. The process of that death resembles something of a spiritual autumn. There are small pieces of us—pieces of sin and distance, pieces of grudge and negligence—that need to die and fall to the earth.

What if leaves never fell? If trees just grew more and more and more, branches upon branches, until their boughs broke? That's not how God designed them. They need to shake off the old leaves to make way for the new; old plants must die so fresh ones can appear in their place, bringing new life and oxygen into our atmosphere. Without death, we would have no new life.

In a way, death is the strategy our earth uses in order to embrace life more fully.

And what if Jesus had never died? We could easily say that the women who wept while Jesus carried his Cross in Luke 23:27–28 were in a deep spiritual fall, recognizing the death of what they had known and deeply believed to be true. Things must have seemed hopeless as they were confronted with the face of death. When they cried out for their Lord and he lay in a cold tomb, they must have felt that death so acutely. We as Catholics do not fear death. We understand its power. We know the end of the story that the women who wept for Jesus did not. We know that with death there comes new life. For us, the death of those things that hinder our spiritual lives brings new life in the form of a deep, intentional relationship with Jesus, being united with him in his kingdom. But first, we have to be willing to let death happen.

WINTER

I loathe winter.

I'm sorry. I know some love it—the beautiful sight of glimmering snow, the smell of pine trees decorated with twinkling lights. I know I'm supposed to talk about how all seasons have their time, but you guys, winter in the Midwest can feel like long, painful torture. A Midwest winter is children arguing over hats and not being able to play outside; it's feeling the icy wind punch you in the face as you step out to get the mail; it's getting up before the sun to shovel heavy loads of white mush off your driveway, almost slipping on the ice.

But while I don't love the actual, earth-identified winter, I've come to embrace the idea of spiritual winters.

During a spiritual winter, you may feel as if Jesus is far away from you. This is the way gardeners feel: when they look out over a desolate yard, it seems as if there's no way anything can truly be under the ground.

Tina Augustine, a friend from my missionary days who continues to do mission work abroad, said she felt as if she encountered a season of spiritual winter right after having kids: "So many days, my heart just said, 'Jesus, are you there? I can't find you.' It was so hard to adjust being a mom and finding any time."

I know I've felt my own spiritual winters. For me, it was transitioning out of my missionary days and into a regular 9-to-5 job. When you spend your days talking to people about Jesus, planning retreats that you truly believe will have an impact on people's spiritual lives, it's hard to transition to sitting in meetings about social media analytics. I felt as if my entire mission in life was suddenly just to bring home a paycheck, when before it had been so much more. I'd pray and not really feel anything in response. Lamentations reads, "How solitary sits the city, once filled with people. She who was great among the nations is now like a widow" (Lam 1:1). That's how I felt: solitary.

Kelly Schroeder, who runs an Etsy shop out of Louisville, Kentucky, suffers from multiple autoimmune diseases, including Hashimoto's disease. She told me that winter for her was made of questions: Why wasn't God healing her? Where *was* he?

But here's a secret about winter, sister: in winter, there is growth.

We cannot see it, but within the bark of those trees, things are shifting and changing. Deep beneath the ground, the plants rest, knowing that soon they will be called upon to radically reach toward the sky. There is so much happening we can't see. The same way we ask where the flowers are in winter, we ask where God is, and there he is: just below the surface, waiting on a timing we do not understand.

If you are in a season of winter, friends and family may be concerned. Maybe you aren't at all of the parties, you aren't volunteering at your church, and you see someone at the grocery store and simply smile instead of engaging them in conversation the way you otherwise would. You know your season: it is one for quiet, inner transformation, not the flashiness of blooming flowers.

And here is the other secret: winter is necessary.

God does not demand that plants bloom, bloom, bloom, constantly showing off, constantly transforming. Neither does he demand the same of us. He knows we need time to pull blankets to our chins and sit with tea, nestled in the peace of knowing that God is God, no matter how we feel. He knows we need time to grow in hidden ways, whether we can see them or not.

In a spiritual winter, here is what we should do: lean into the season. I think we try to rush through our literal and metaphorical winters. Writer Lara Casey has often described the importance of waiting to plant until it's time. She writes on her blog, "Now, let me tell you, I have ignored this recommendation several times. And every time I've regretted it. In our area, the weather gets lovely in late February and March is magical, and it makes everyone want to plant things right away. But wise gardeners know to be patient. I've gotten over-eager a time or two and planted tomatoes in March only to have to dig them out before a freeze and give them a temporary abode in my kitchen. Be patient in planting, my fellow gardeners. You'll be glad you waited."[2]

Winter is a time of waiting, a time of returning to our roots. This may be the time to call up your old friend who always has solid spiritual wisdom for you, who has served as your touchstone in the past. Perhaps it's time to return to that spiritual read that always reminds you of the risen Lord. Maybe it's time to just sit—sit in silence or with Audrey Assad playing in the background, and let your simple prayers be enough. Because they *are*, sister. They are.

It's also, for part of winter, the season of Advent: a literal waiting for the birth of our Lord. Caryll Houselander writes in *The Reed of God*, "Advent is the season of the seed: Christ loved this symbol of the seed. The seed, He said, is the Word of God sown in the human heart."[3] Oftentimes, spiritual winters are times of rest in preparation for the busy spring to follow. Trying to rush through and get to the next step will be a disservice to ourselves in the end. The seed hasn't yet been planted, but it's there, in our hearts, whether or not we feel it.

There is a time for every season.

It's easy to look at the seasons and think that spring or summer are obviously the greatest. But just like our ever-turning world, we are in need of all of the seasons.

We cannot live in perpetual spiritual summer, just as we cannot live in perpetual spiritual winter. Our lives are not always going to be booming, blooming, and bursting at the seams. Sometimes they are quiet, and the look is more *hygge*: tea, twinkling lights, and a true, uninterrupted rest. Sometimes they are full of death before the resurrection. Sometimes they look anything but beautiful.

We cannot stay in any one season. Seasons are made for a time. They begin, and then they end, and we walk forward.

Here's what we need to remember:

Blooming is taking place.

It's taking place in every season; *it just looks different.*

You can bloom in the depths of winter, you can bloom in the planting of spring, you can bloom in the joy of summer, and you can bloom in the reaping of autumn.

Your circumstances are different than mine, but that spiritual truth does not change.

Some may fear winter. Summer, after all, is so much more fun. But Isaiah writes to us, "Do not . . . fear what they fear, nor feel dread" (Is 8:12). We should not fear what the world fears. We will not fear death or the cold; we will guard our houses against the snow. Remember, "The LORD is close to the brokenhearted and saves those who are crushed in spirit" (Ps 34:18, NIV).

Your season is different than mine, but you have been planted in the earth by an all-powerful Jesus, and I claim his name over your season so that you may have the fullness of life.

Just as Isaiah says, "The wilderness and the parched land will exult; the Arabah will rejoice and bloom; Like the crocus it shall bloom abundantly, and rejoice with joyful song. . . . They will see the glory of the LORD, the splendor of our God" (Is 35:1–2).

SOUL-CARE STEPS

* **Identify your season.** This will help you embrace a way of living out your spirituality that feels most natural in this moment of time. Remember, we don't want to rush through seasons—they're all important. Don't strive for spring if you feel like you're in the middle of winter. Instead, try and seek out what your spiritual winter is trying to teach you by meeting with a spiritual director or implementing a new prayer routine. If you're in a more joyful season, such as summer, embrace it! Don't sit around being anxious about when your feelings of consolation might leave.

* **Make a list of what's working and what's not.** This sounds incredibly basic, but I've found it a helpful practice. Make a list of what's working right now and what's not. Maybe making homemade organic dinners for your family every night is bringing you a sweet sense of joy, or maybe you're getting completely stressed out and need to order in some Blue Apron. Maybe there's a friendship or relationship that's run its course and needs a painful goodbye. Maybe your commute to work every day just feels like trudging through mud and you need a new podcast to listen to. These things can be big, small, or anywhere in between, but sitting and making a list can help us move toward tangible answers instead of just trying to feel our way through things.

* **Be kind to yourself.** This is so much easier said than done. But if you're in a hard, dark season, you may need to step away from your Bible study or marathon training. And that's fine. Don't beat yourself up. Take care of yourself in the most practical, thoughtful, science-proven ways you can: drink water, exercise, pray, and log off the laptop. These small, tactile health motions can add up to a lighter burden. And if you're in a season of joy and sunshine, it's also important not to forget he who is giving it to you and to take care of your body while rejoicing in his grace.

Conclusion

Once upon a time, a girl knew it all.

Then, God.

Is this not the story of all of our lives? The story of the Israelites, the story of Mary Magdalene, the story of all who have come into contact with the risen Lord?

God is here, on whatever holy ground you're standing on, making all things new.

It probably doesn't feel like it. I get that. You wake up and are in the same ugly apartment with the same dull job; you're still not in the vocation you've been dreaming about, or maybe you're in it and it's nothing like you dreamed. You pictured motherhood one way and were handed infertility or kids with special needs or co-parenting with a former spouse. Or maybe you even got the motherhood you wanted, but it came with more poopy diapers , tantrums, and postpartum depression than you expected. You asked for medical school and were served a heaping pile of wait list. You started a nonprofit that crumbled; you launched a business that failed.

And yet here you are: you are doing it. You are breathing in and out; you are seeking the Word of God.

You are already blooming, because you are already trying.

This is what blooming looks like: not the hard-won finished product of a beautiful peony, but the grit and grace of growth. If you're trying to thrive in your current season, you're blooming. If you're looking for the light, you're blooming.

It's so tempting to look around at our sisters and see the ways in which they're blooming but we're not. But different flowers bloom on different schedules: snowdrops spring up at the first sight of spring and peonies take months to finally open up and smile at the sun. So too we, the daughters of Christ, are not just one flower, and we don't all bloom at the same time or in the same ways.

I hesitated to do the whole garden-metaphor thing because so often when women are compared to flowers, it's to say they're fragile. Pretty. Mostly around for decoration.

But the people who see a garden and think that its main feature is beauty are missing out. Yes, gardens can come in gorgeous colors and please our eyes. But they can also feed us, they require us to get our hands dirty, and they teach us about life. It can take hours of toiling before they're where you want them. They can literally sustain our bodies.

There's a place called Svalbard located right between Norway and the North Pole. When you look at pictures of it, it looks like something out of a fantasy novel: a huge spread of ice with reindeer dotting the horizon. Its average temperature in the winter is between 3 and 10 degrees Fahrenheit. It's a frozen tundra of snow and crystal.

But in the middle of Svalbard, there's a giant greenhouse: the Svalbard Global Seed Vault. Inside the vault are thousands of seeds of various plants. The entire world has collaborated on this vault, making sure it can hold varieties of flowers and vegetation. The seeds kept there are meant to sustain the world in case of a global crisis. When we eventually ruin the planet or blow everyone up in some fit of violence and vicious pride, we will have these seeds to turn to. We will be able to plant them and start again.

Albert Camus once wrote that in the depths of winter we have within us "an invincible summer." Just like in Svalbard, a winter wonderland of ice, we have infinite blooming potential within ourselves. In the deepest freeze, we have the potential to start again.

There is one final step in this process, and that is an incredible leap of faith. We so often think that faith is something that will suddenly burst up if we shut our eyes tightly enough or listen to breathy praise and worship music at high volumes. We give into the "name it, claim it" subculture of Christian evangelicalism, thinking that if we simply ask enough times (after all, aren't we supposed to be the persistent widow of Luke 18?!) Jesus will grant us our wishes like some sort of magical genie. As if the point of faith was getting what we want—as if it wasn't a relationship, a give-and-take of pure love.

We forget that faith is something that must be diligently tended to and that it has seasons, some that feel impossible. When you hold a packet of seeds in your hand, it's easy to think, *What kind of miracle is going to transform these into tomatoes?*

This sense of faith can only come from knowing this: that Christ died for you and that through him all things are possible.

Our Jesus is a God who knows loss. The guy they talk about at megachurches who wants us all to be rich and comfortable and powerful on earth? I'm not sure who they're chatting about, but that isn't *my* Jesus, the miracle worker who hung on a Cross. Because that guy promised we would be taken where we did not want to go. And we are in that place. But as St. John Paul II said,

> It is Jesus that you seek when you dream of happiness;
> He is waiting for you when nothing else you find satis-
> fies you; He is the beauty to which you are so attracted;
> it is He who provoked you with that thirst for fullness
> that will not let you settle for compromise; it is He who
> urges you to shed the masks of a false life; it is He who
> reads in your heart your most genuine choices, the
> choices that others try to stifle. It is Jesus who stirs in
> you the desire to do something great with your lives, the
> will to follow an ideal, the refusal to allow yourselves to
> be ground down by mediocrity, the courage to commit
> yourselves humbly and patiently to improving your-
> selves and society, making the world more human and
> more fraternal.[1]

As I write this conclusion, it is Advent. I have a half-hearted wreath crafted in the corner of our living room and *Advent Story-book* laying at my feet, ready for my two toddlers to flip through. It's morning, and my coffee is hot. Every single Sunday right now we are singing "O Come, O Come, Emmanuel" as the priest pro-ceeds down the aisle. *Emmanuel* means "God with us," so we are essentially asking Jesus to come so that God can be with us. Good news, sisters: he came. He is with us. Emmanuel is here, among us, in the "pots and pans" St. Teresa of Avila spoke about, in the dark nights experienced by Mother Teresa, in every crack and corner of our days. You are not alone because God is here, and so are we.

Way back in chapter 3, I said we were all united. This community you're seeking already exists; it is the living, breathing Body of Christ. It is our souls and the Spirit. Connected through the Eucharist, all of us, blooming together.

I'm going to get a little old-school campus missionary on you, now. Don't freak out. Here we go. I'm going to pray over you.

I pray you be filled with courage. The courage to admit that the season you are in may be one of winter, of icy storms, of broken and bleeding knuckles cracked from the frigid earth. I pray you are able to open your mouth and say this truth.

I pray you heal from people in the Church who have hurt and offended and broken, relying on the Spirit to glue you back together before turning and helping others do the same.

I pray you find God in unlikely places, be it emergency rooms or lonely nights or a cold gray cubicle. I pray you lift the muddy rocks on your own porch to see the beautiful earth beneath.

I pray you are able to set up boundaries, to protect your own garden from wolves in sheep's clothing.

I pray you find Jesus, entirely: not just a snippet of him here, a quote he said there, a command he gave to this group, or something he mentioned to that one, but his whole self. I pray you develop the type of relationship with him that lasts, one with a foundation that doesn't crumble.

I pray you choose with confidence and grace.

May the road rise up to meet you.

Go forth. Peace be with you.

Acknowledgments

Thank you, as always, to Amber Elder. Your kindness, expertise, and dedication have made this book what it is. Thank you, also, to the rest of the team at Ave Maria Press.

Eternal gratitude to the listeners and guests of *The Catholic Feminist* podcast. Thank you for allowing me to be in your earbuds and on your bookshelves.

I'm so grateful for our church community, St. Dominic, and the friends there who feel like family. To my goddaughter, Ellie Lawton—I hope one day these words mean something to you.

Without my mastermind sisters, I would have lost my mind over the past year, so thank you times a thousand to Jenny Parulski, Shannon Ochoa, Mallory Smyth, Erica Comitalo, Sam Povlock, and Emily Runyan. And to Emily Linn, Megan Stram, and Terri Meyerhofer—thank you for giving recipes and, most importantly, for being there.

I've been greatly influenced by many priests in my life, but I need to particularly shout out Fr. John Gibson and Fr. Eric Sternberg for being not just wonderful spiritual mentors but also dear friends.

Thank you to my parents and siblings, who have supported me in moments that were anything but thriving. You taught me to bloom in chaos and seek the sun always, and for that, I can never say thank you enough.

I would be nothing but a weed without my husband, Krzys, and my children, Benjamin and Teresa. You three are the greatest flowers in my garden. I love you infinitely.

And God: you don't need my thanks. But I sing it anyway.

Appendix: Recipes

I know that in chapter 6 I said a lot about cooking for people, but look: you can just order pizza. Nobody here is judging you an ounce, and if it's your cooking skills that are stopping you from inviting people into your home, then you pick up your phone and pull up Grubhub. But I *truly* believe you can cook, okay? It's not that hard. Recipes are just sets of instructions. I can't put together an IKEA desk, but I can make a risotto, and if I can, you can. If you can read, which you can because you're reading this book, then you can make some basic food for people. Furthermore, I've served people burned chicken and spaghetti sauce from a can, and you know what? *Nobody died.* You've got this.

I wanted to share some simple recipes from me and a few of my ride-or-die friends that you can serve to people in a pinch. You'll notice that with mine, I'm all about doing things "to taste"—a cup or more, a sprinkle of this, a dash of that. Because I think food, like the people you're making it for, is different for each of us. The best way to cook is to cook by trying things over and over again. But that's what's great about cooking; it's pretty hard to mess up. You'll get better as you go and experiment along the way. These are recipes we make for the people we love. I share them because when we feed one another, we are feeding Christ.

Sourdough Bread

EMILY LINN

Note from Emily: This recipe takes a little tender love and care and patience to perfect. But if you get the hang of it, bread making can truly be an art. Fresh bread to share with a little olive oil and balsamic vinegar warms the heart, is great for filling you up over conversation on the couch, and is good paired with red wine. My husband and I use this recipe weekly (or more) for when we have people over for dinner, hang out, watch football (go Packers!), or simply bake our family's daily bread (second to Jesus, obviously). We have ventured out and tried other recipes such as sourdough pancakes, English muffins, biscuits, and pizza dough. The thing we love about sourdough is once you have a good starter, it is something that you can share with others to pass on the deliciousness!

A FEW KEY ITEMS THAT ARE GOOD TO INVEST IN IF YOU ARE SERIOUS ABOUT BREAD MAKING

Sourdough starter: We obtained our starter from a Jesuit friend who has great wisdom about bread. He is our master; we are his bread disciples. I suggest asking around, looking on Facebook Marketplace, etc. I have had friends try to make their own starter from scratch; however, I have not heard many success stories from this method. What even is a starter? That is a great question. It is fermented dough containing yeast and bacteria that help the bread to rise. (The process of growing your sourdough starter is similar in some ways to fermenting kombucha, cheese, beer, sauerkraut, or other fermented foods and drinks.)

Kitchen scale: This is key if you would like your bread loaves to be consistent. Different flour can vary in volume, making your measurement in cups vary. A scale helps you stay consistent by measuring mass instead.

Dutch oven: Cooks a beautiful, browned loaf!

Standing KitchenAid mixer with a bread hook: For easy kneading.

SOURDOUGH STARTER TIPS

You have to feed your sourdough starter every day *or* split it and use half to make your dough. How do you feed it? Mix 1/2 cup flour and 1/2 cup water into the starter. It *should* be goopy! Getting tired of feeding your starter every day? If you place it in the fridge, your starter will "hibernate." I am not sure how long you can leave your starter in the fridge; we have left it in there for two weeks before. When you hibernate your starter, make sure that it is fed and has had time to "eat" (absorb the new flour and water) before placing it in the fridge; otherwise, you are stopping the eating process before the starter has had time to feast!

If you're getting liquid on the top of your starter, that means alcohol is being created as a byproduct of the starter eating the flour. This liquid means that your starter is hungry (and getting boozy). Simply drain the alcohol off the top and feed your starter.

INGREDIENTS

2 tsp yeast
460 mL water
800 g unbleached flour
320 g *unfed* sourdough starter
10 g salt

DIRECTIONS

It's about six o'clock in the evening, a perfect time to prep your bread dough!

In a spouted measuring cup, mix 78.9 mL (1/3 cup) warm water with 2 tsp of yeast. Set this mixture aside. Let it do its thing for about 4 minutes.

In a big mixing bowl (or a KitchenAid standing mixer bowl), measure out the flour, unfed starter, and salt.

Add in the yeast-water mixture and the remaining water.

Knead the mixture by hand or use a mixer to bring everything together. If using a standing mixer, mix on low for 6–7 minutes until all the flour is incorporated and the mixture does not leave residue on the sides of the bowl when mixing.

Place a towel over the mixture for approximately 3 hours or until the dough doubles in size. (Note: This recipe makes either one big loaf or two smaller loaves. If you decide to make two loaves, this is the time to split the mixture.)

After 3 hours, punch your dough down and slightly knead it (in a folding motion), shaping one sturdy loaf.

Heavily flour a different bowl and transfer your dough to this bowl (you can even line the bowl with a towel and flour the towel; this helps for easy transfer from the bowl to the Dutch oven for baking).

Place a towel over the dough and let it sit overnight in the refrigerator. The dough should sit at least 8 hours but not more than 24 hours.

In the morning, preheat the oven to 450 degrees Fahrenheit.

Line the bottom of the Dutch oven with parchment paper.

Place the prepared dough in the Dutch oven and, with a knife, score a cross on the top of the dough. This will help air escape from the dough while cooking and cooling, and it makes the end product look very pretty.

Cook with the lid on for 20 minutes, then take the lid off and allow to cook for 10 more minutes. (Taking the lid off creates the nice browning of the bread.)

Enjoy!

Wonton Stars

MEGAN STRAM

Note from Megan: Some of my earliest memories are of running around with my cousins at my great-grandparents' house. No matter how recently I had eaten, I was immediately hungry when I walked into that house, and there was always something delicious to eat there. Stars were a common option. When I was a teenager, my cousin taught me how to make them, and ever since then they have been my go-to for all sorts of gatherings.

I recently made them for a weekend cabin getaway with friends. As we began to prepare dinner one evening, we had three people using the stove all at once. It was a bit chaotic. One of my friends offered to help, so I tasked her with cutting up the green peppers. Another friend stirred the meat while I worked on mixing everything else up. Recipes like this one allow cooking to be a group effort. I love that. They provide opportunities for generosity, foster communication, and are so much fun! As each batch of wontons came out of the oven, it was plated and then immediately passed around the group, which resulted in a plate emptied and ready for the next batch to come out.

INGREDIENTS

Wonton wrappers (found in the produce section of most grocery stores)
1 lb pork sausage
2 cups shredded cheddar cheese, separated
1 green bell pepper, finely diced

1 can chopped black olives
1 1/2 tbsp dry ranch mix
1/2 cup mayonnaise
1/3 cup milk

DIRECTIONS

Preheat the oven to 400 degrees.

Over medium heat, brown the pork sausage.

Once the sausage has browned, mix it together with 1 3/4 cups of the cheddar cheese, bell pepper, chopped black olives, dry ranch mix, mayonnaise, and milk.

Spray the muffin tin with cooking spray.

Place one wonton wrapper into each individual cavity in the muffin tin.

Once the oven has preheated, bake the empty shells for 4 minutes.

Fill each shell with equal portions of the sausage mixture.

Bake for an additional 4 minutes.

Remove the wontons from the tin and place them on a serving platter.

Sprinkle a pinch of the remaining 1/4 cup cheddar cheese over each star.

Repeat placing wonton wrappers and filling them until all the filling is used.

Stuffed Vienna Bread

TERRI MEYERHOFER

Note from Terri: My mom has made this recipe countless times for family gatherings and other parties; it is an often-requested dish. Sometimes she makes half of it without mushrooms so that my dad will eat it. I have many memories of helping her make this and then making it by myself in my college apartment. Something about a mom's touch always makes it taste better, though!

INGREDIENTS

1 loaf Vienna bread, not sliced
1 lb Swiss cheese, grated
8 oz fresh mushrooms, coarsely chopped
3 green onions, sliced thin horizontally with stems included and then cut in half vertically
2 tbsp poppy seeds or sesame seeds
1 tsp seasoned salt (I use Lawry's)
1 cup butter
1 1/2 tsp lemon juice
1 tbsp dry mustard

DIRECTIONS

Preheat the oven to 350 degrees Fahrenheit.

Cut the bread from top to bottom, stopping 1/2 inch from the bottom. Make the cuts 1 inch apart and cut both horizontally and vertically. When you're looking at the bread from the top, you want to have created a grid pattern with 1 inch by 1 inch squares. The bottom side of the bread shouldn't be cut.

Stuff each bread section* with the cheese, the mushrooms, and half of the onions. When you stuff the bread, it will pull apart a little and open up like a blooming onion.

Sprinkle the remaining onion, poppy/sesame seeds, and seasoned salt over the top.

Melt the butter. Add the lemon juice and dry mustard to the melted butter. Stir to dissolve.

Gently pour the butter mixture over the bread.*

Wrap the bread in foil and bake at 350 degrees Fahrenheit for 40 minutes. Let cool, then unwrap the foil and serve.

*Stuffing the bread can be done earlier; however, wait to pour the butter over the bread until right before baking.

Easy Crock-Pot Broccoli Cheddar Soup

CLAIRE SWINARSKI

Note from Claire: Anything you can make in a Crock-Pot is terrific for hosting because you don't have to keep chopping and stirring when guests arrive. I also love this as a meal for new moms, particularly during Lent: it's hearty and warm and inviting, all without meat, making it affordable, too. This is not for our dairy-free friends, but I'm from Wisconsin, where cheese is an art form. Pair it with Emily's sourdough bread and knock someone's socks off.

INGREDIENTS

1 lb frozen broccoli florets
1 medium-sized onion, chopped
2 whole carrots, chopped
4 cups chicken broth
1 cup water
1/2 teaspoon salt

1/2 teaspoon pepper
2 cans cream of celery soup (I use Campbell's, but you can get fancy and organic if that's your jam)
1 1/2 lb Velveeta (again, I'm not a fancy lady, clearly)
2 cups sharp cheddar cheese, grated

DIRECTIONS

Throw everything *except* the Velveeta and cheddar cheese in the Crock-Pot on low and let that baby simmer.

After about four hours, throw the mixture in a blender (carefully, it's hot!) or use an immersion blender and blend until it's nice and creamy.

If you used a blender, return the soup to the Crock-Pot.

Then add the cheeses to the soup and let it melt; it will only take about 20 minutes before it's ready to serve.

I add a bunch more salt and a dash of hot sauce after the cheeses have melted and before serving, but you do you. That's what's great about soup; it's easy to personalize and anyone can make it. My kids go crazy when I serve it with oyster crackers.

Date-Night-In Brie and Berries

CLAIRE SWINARSKI

Note from Claire: My husband and I love, love, love food. Our favorite date nights involve new-to-us restaurants where we order such an oddly large amount of food that the waiter asks if we're expecting other people to join us. But with two toddlers, we've tweaked our date nights so that they mostly involve a rented movie and our basement.

However, we still try to keep our date nights in meaningful by jazz-ing them up a bit. This is our all-time favorite fancy snack. It's easy to make, but it always impresses people, making it perfect for a date night in, a girl's night, or a book club.

INGREDIENTS

1 wheel of extra creamy brie cheese
1/4 cup of water
1 lb cranberries
1 cup (more or less to taste) of sugar
Crackers of choice
Honey

DIRECTIONS

Preheat your oven to 350 degrees Fahrenheit.

Once preheated, bake your brie for around 8 minutes. You want it to be *just* warm enough that it's oozing slightly, but not so warm that it melts and bursts open.

While the brie is baking, take your cranberries, water, and sugar (start with 3/4 cup, then add more to taste) and heat them in a pot on the stovetop, stirring frequently, to make a tangy cranberry sauce.

Once your cheese is ready, pull it out of the oven, pour your sauce over the top, and drizzle the whole thing with as much honey as you'd like.

I honestly believe this is best paired with good ol' down-home Ritz crackers, but if you want to get fancy, some sea salt or olive oil crackers would work well, too.

Notes

INTRODUCTION

1. Shannon K. Evans, "Everyday Ignatian: Imitating Mary's Motherhood Calls Me to a Life of Justice," *Jesuits News Detail*, January 21, 2020, https://jesuits.org/news-detail?TN=NEWS-20191017013747USAUSAUSA.

2. "Pope: Sad Christian faces are like pickled peppers," *Catholic News Agency*, May 10, 2013, https://www.catholicnewsagency.com/news/pope-sad-christian-faces-are-like-pickled-peppers. Emphasis added.

1. STUCK IN THE MUD

1. You can read more about that in my first book, *Girl, Arise!: A Catholic Feminist's Invitation to Live Boldly, Love Your Faith, and Change the World* (Notre Dame, IN: Ave Maria Press, 2019).

2. *Trial of Nullification of Joan of Arc*, 1449–1455 AD, Testimony of Duke Jean d'Alençon from the examination at Poitiers, cited in Etienne Robo, *The Holiness of St. Joan of Arc* (London: Catholic Truth Society, 1951). See http://www.stjoan-center.com/Trials/null07.html.

3. Pope Francis (@Pontifex), "We cannot be tepid disciples. The Church needs our courage in order to give witness to truth," Twitter, March 25, 2014, 11:25 a.m., https://twitter.com/pontifex/status/448405224655298560?lang=en.

2. LOOKING UNDER THE SOIL

1. St. Augustine, "Homily VII," in *A Select Library of the Nicene and Post-Nicene Fathers of the Christian Church*, ed. Philip Schaff, series 1, vol. 7, *St. Augustin: Homilies on the Gospel of John; Homilies on the First Epistle of John; Soliloquies* (Edinburgh: T&T Clark, n.d.), https://www.ccel.org/ccel/schaff/npnf107.iv.x.html.

3. DEVELOPING GOOD ROUTINES

1. Sarah Mackenzie, *The Read-Aloud Family: Making Meaningful and Lasting Connections with Your Kids* (Grand Rapids: Zondervan, 2018), 53.

2. Henry Cloud and John Townsend, *Boundaries: When to Say Yes, How to Say No to Take Control of Your Life* (Grand Rapids: Zondervan, 1992), 37.

3. "Meet the Generation That Volunteers the Most," Up with People Volunteer Abroad, January 11, 2018, https://upwithpeople.org/uwp-blog/meet-generation-volunteers/.

4. Brené Brown, "Jesus Wept," The Work of the People, Facebook, March 19, 2016, https://www.facebook.com/watch/?v=1015401132 7415682.

4. PLANTING A PERSPECTIVE

1. Jen Hatmaker, *Of Mess and Moxie: Wrangling Delight Out of This Wild and Glorious Life* (Nashville, TN: Thomas Nelson, 2017), 20.

2. Hatmaker, *Of Mess and Moxie*, 24.

3. Jemar Tisby, *The Color of Compromise: The Truth about the American Church's Complicity in Racism* (Grand Rapids: Zondervan, 2019).

4. "Giving thanks can make you happier," HEALTHbeat, Harvard Health Publishing, https://www.health.harvard.edu/healthbeat/giving-thanks-can-make-you-happier.

5. PUTTING DOWN ROOTS

1. "Anthony Bourdain as Interviewed by Nathan Thornburgh," SXSW, April 19, 2016, YouTube video, 46:35, https://www.youtube.com/watch?v=ZVtOIXwFu5o.

6. PLANTING FELLOWSHIP

1. Junno Arocho Esteves, "Christian community a place of welcome, solidarity, pope says," *National Catholic Reporter*, June 26, 2019, https://www.ncronline.org/news/vatican/francis-chronicles/christian-community-place-welcome-solidarity-pope-says.

2. Shauna Niequist, *Bread and Wine: A Love Letter to Life around the Table with Recipes* (Grand Rapids: Zondervan, 2013), 4.

3. Mary Karr, "Disgraceland," *Poetry* (January 2004): https://www.poetryfoundation.org/poetrymagazine/poems/42065/disgraceland.

7. HAPPY FOR NOW VS. JOY ETERNAL

1. Maria Faustina Kowalska, *Diary: Divine Mercy in My Soul* (Stockbridge, MA: Marian Press, 2005), 86, part 153.

2. "Kanye West Airpool Karaoke," *The Late Late Show with James Corden*, October 29, 2019, https://www.youtube.com/watch?v=vgLOv36an3s.

3. John Paul II, "Seventeenth World Youth Day Papal Welcoming Ceremony Address," Exhibition Place, Toronto, July 25, 2002, http://www.vatican.va/content/john-paul-ii/en/speeches/2002/july/documents/hf_jp-ii_spe_20020725_wyd-address-youth.html.

4. Caryll Houselander, *The Reed of God*, rev. ed. (Notre Dame, IN: Christian Classics, 2006), 66.

5. "Giving thanks can make you happier," HEALTHbeat, Harvard Health Publishing, https://www.health.harvard.edu/healthbeat/giving-thanks-can-make-you-happier.

8. EMBRACING THE SEASONS

1. DuBose Heyward, "Summertime," in George Gershwin, *Porgy and Bess* (New York: Gershwin Publishing, 1935).

2. Lara Casey, "Gardening 101, Part 1: The Story of an Unlikely Gardener," *Lara Casey* (blog), February 23, 2017, https://laracasey.com/2017/02/23/gardening-101-part-1-the-story-of-an-unlikely-gardener/.

3. Houselander, *Reed of God*, 55.

CONCLUSION

1. John Paul II, "15th World Youth Day Vigil of Prayer," Tor Vergata, August 19, 2000, http://w2.vatican.va/content/john-paul-ii/en/speeches/2000/jul-sep/documents/hf_jp-ii_spe_20000819_gmg-veglia.html.

Claire Swinarski is the author of books for both adults and children, including *Girl, Arise!* A former FOCUS missionary and University of Wisconsin Badger, Swinarski's work has been featured in *Radiant* magazine, Blessed Is She, FemCatholic, *The Washington Post, Good Housekeeping, Seventeen, Verily, America*, and many other publications. She's also the host of *The Catholic Feminist* podcast, a top-ranked spirituality show with almost two million downloads. She lives outside of Milwaukee, Wisconsin, with her husband and two children.

www.thecatholicfeministpodcast.com
Facebook: thecatholicfeministpodcast
Instagram: @thecatholicfeminist